NOTEWORTHY

Listening and Notetaking Skills

SECOND EDITION

Phyllis L. Lim
University of Arizona

William Smalzer

Heinle & Heinle Publishers
I(T)P   An International Thomson Publishing Company

Pacific Grove • Albany • Bonn • Boston • Cincinnati • Detroit • London • Madrid • Melbourne
Mexico City • New York • Paris • San Francisco • Tokyo • Toronto • Washington

The Publication of *Noteworthy, Second Edition* was directed by the members of the Newbury House Publishing Team at Heinle & Heinle:

Erik Gundersen, *Editorial Director*
John F. McHugh, *Market Development Director*
Kristin Thalheimer, *Production Services Coordinator*

Also participating in the publication of this program were:

Publisher: Stanley J. Galek
Director of Production: Elizabeth Holthaus
Project Manager: Linda Lee
Senior Assistant Editor: Ken Pratt
Manufacturing Coordinator: Mary Beth Hennebury
Photo Researcher: Phillippe Heckly
Photo/Video Specialist: Jonathan Stark
Interior Text Designer: Carol H. Rose
Cover Artist: Patty Yehle, The Fringe
Cover Designer: Gina Petti, Rotunda Design

LIBRARY OF CONGRESS CATALOGING-IN-PUBLICATION DATA

Lim, Phyllis L.
    Noteworthy : listening and notetaking skills / Phyllis L. Lim,
William Smalzer
    p.   cm.
    ISBN 0-8384-5009-1
    1. English language—Textbooks for foreign speakers. 2.
Notetaking—Problems, exercises, etc. 3. Listening—Problems,
exercises, etc. I. Smalzer, William, 1946- . II. Title.
PE1128.L468   1995
428.3'4—dc20
                                           95-49064
                                         CIP

Heinle & Heinle Publishers/A Division of International Thomson Publishing, Inc.

Manufactured in the United States of America

ISBN 0-8384-5009-1

10 9

CONTENTS

UNIT FOUR Education 103

UNIT FIVE The Official Side 139

PREFACE

NOTEWORTHY is a high-intermediate to advanced level ESL/EFL listening and notetaking program with three major goals:

1. to improve listening comprehension and develop academic notetaking skills through extensive practice

2. to provide foreign students with a deeper, clearer understanding of life and culture in the United States

3. to increase productive skills through tasks in which students use aural input for reproduction and transfer activities in speaking and writing.

Learning new vocabulary is an important part of each lesson, and several important notetaking skills are presented and practiced. However, overall we have used a content approach. The final activity of each unit is a written quiz covering the content of the three lectures in the unit. (Neither the tapescripts nor the quizzes appear in the student book; they are in the *Tapescript and Answer Key*, which accompanies the cassettes.)

The topics of the 15 lectures, divided into five units, are both universal and academic in nature: population, immigration, university life, multiculturalism, technology, education, and government, for example. The vocabulary is mostly subtechnical, found and used across disciplines and in different professions. There is a general progression from easy to more difficult within each unit and from the beginning to the end of the book. The lectures are delivered in a relaxed, natural style of speech.

An effort is made to help students see the organization of a lecture in English, to see both the forest and the trees. Motivation to take good notes is built in, as students need their notes for oral activities soon after the lecture and for a quiz some time later.

Packaged with the cassettes, the *Tapescript and Answer Key* with comprehensive quizzes is available to aid the teacher.

To the Teacher

Teachers will find that NOTEWORTHY offers both stimulating topics for study and great versatility. Any one of its three major goals can be emphasized to fit the needs of different classes. A teacher who chooses not to devote the extra time needed for students to take notes could use the materials for listening comprehension with a focus on cultural content. Individual lessons could be used to provide background for further treatment of a topic, and suggestions for doing so are given. And, of course, the teacher who wishes to concentrate on production could use the lectures as input for the accompanying oral and written exercises.

Note: The symbol ![headphones symbol] in the margin indicates that the material needed to complete the listening activity is on the cassette that accompanies the text. It will be necessary to rewind the cassette to the beginning of the exercise or lecture for a second or third listening of the same material.

New Features in the Second Edition

❍ New topics, including "Americans at Work," "Multiculturalism," "Crime and Violence," and "Technology: The Better Mousetrap," as well as a selection of updated lectures from the first edition.

❍ Extensive work on rhetorical cues to help students detect the organization of the lectures.

❍ Communicative follow-ups to lectures in which students verify their notes by asking each other questions.

❍ Accuracy checks that require students to refer to their notes rather than answer questions from memory.

❍ Transfer activities that accommodate EFL as well as ESL classes.

❍ Collaborative activities for writing summaries and essay question answers as well as for developing critical thinking skills.

❍ Suggestions for pursuing the topic.

❍ Quiz preparation for each unit. Students review lectures and collaborate in writing short-answer and essay exam questions.

❍ Unit quizzes located in the *Tapescript and Answer Key* instead of in the student's book.

Chapter Outline

Provided below is an explanation of the purpose of each part of a full chapter, which requires about three 50-minute periods to complete. (Teachers who opt to do Pursuing the Topic will need additional periods.)

Discussion: to introduce the topic, to stimulate students' curiosity, and to begin establishing a cognitive schema for the lecture through a discussion of illustrations.

Vocabulary and Key Concepts: to familiarize students with new subtechnical vocabulary and with the major concepts of the chapter.

Predictions: to get students to invest in the lesson by predicting the content of the lecture through their questions. As students share their prediction questions with the class, a schema for the content is further established.

Notetaking Preparation: to give students strategies for understanding the organization of lectures and for taking down information in an organized manner and in a meaningful, usable form.

Listening: to lead students through a series of listenings to distinguish the main subtopics from supporting details. Some guidance is given, but content is stressed over skills, and the emphasis is on repeated practice at notetaking.

Accuracy Check: to check students' comprehension and the completeness of their notes through a ten-question short-answer quiz.

Oral Activities: to provide small-group oral practice that draws on the language and information of the lecture as input to improve students' oral competence. At the same time, students check the completeness of their notes, which they use for these activities.

Review: reconstruction of different portions of the lecture.

Transfer: questions for discussion or for an oral report on a similar topic in the students' countries.

Collaboration: to provide opportunities for students to further develop language and academic skills in small groups through discussion, summary writing, and writing answers to essay questions.

Pursuing the Topic: to offer suggestions for further study of the topic through readings, videos, and interviews.

Unit Quiz Preparation (at the end of each unit): to help students anticipate unit quiz questions by reviewing notes in order to distinguish main ideas from supporting ones. Students write quiz questions and answer them.

Unit Quiz (in the *Tapescript and Answer Key*): to evaluate students' mastery of the skills/content taught and to simulate the college/university experience of taking a test on content. Quizzes require both short answers and essay answers.

Suggestions for Teaching

Discussion: Question students briefly about the photographs to get them to focus on them and to enter the topic. Then discuss the questions as a class. Write important vocabulary on the board, if time permits. The activity should require no more than a few minutes, just enough time to introduce the topic and arouse curiosity. Time: 4–5 minutes.

Vocabulary and Key Concepts: Have students quickly read through the sentences silently before they listen to the dictated sentences on the tape. This encourages students to invest in the exercise and may be done as homework. After they listen to the tape and fill in the blanks, quickly go over the spelling of each word, and discuss the meanings of words they ask about. Time: 10–12 minutes.

Predictions: Ask students to write three questions about the possible content of the lecture so that they make more of an investment in the lesson. If the example questions aren't enough to get them started writing their own questions, ask a "leading" question or two: Do you know how many people there are in the United States? (Pause) How would you write the question to find out? Time: 8–10 minutes.

Notetaking Preparation: Go over the skill in Section D.1 and have students practice the skill if appropriate. Try to move quickly, since they will practice the skill again during the lecture. Some skill exercises could also be assigned as homework, and those that require prelecture reading should be. Section D.2, which generally deals with the organization of the lecture, can be done as homework and checked in class to save time. Time: will vary depending on the particular skill in D.1 and whether D.2 is done in class or at home.

Listening: The text calls for two listenings per lecture and additional listening outside of class for those students who fail to get at least 70% on the Accuracy Check. There is nothing magical in these numbers. Students stronger in listening comprehension may do well with fewer listenings from the beginning, and weaker students may need more, especially at the beginning of the course. Take into account the general level of the class when deciding how many whole-class listenings to do. Try to maintain some pressure without pushing students to the frustration level. If possible, provide an opportunity for additional listening *outside* class. Ideally, in one class period, you should get through at least the Prelistening Activities and the First Listening. Time: depends on the length of each lecture and the number of listenings done in class. (Actual lecture times vary from about 7 minutes to about 12 minutes.)

Accuracy Check: Do as quickly as is feasible. After students listen to and answer questions by referring to their notes, discuss only those answers that students disagree on. Try to raise their consciousness about why they missed an answer: Did they misunderstand the lecture? Were their notes inaccurate? Or were they unable to locate the information in their notes? Sometimes students try to write down too much and miss relevant information. Sometimes they may simply be unable to locate information that they have in their notes. Recommendations for further listening and/or rewriting notes should be made at this time. Strive to complete and discuss the Accuracy Check by the end of the second class. Time: 12–15 minutes.

Oral Activities:

Review: Be sure that every student is involved in the by having individual students responsible for assigned sections of the lecture. (If students get their "assignments" the previous day, they can prepare at home and save class time.) You can vary the activity by having pairs or small groups of students prepare the same section together. Sometimes you may want individual students to report on their sections to just one other student; at other times, pairs or small groups can report to the whole class. Time: 10–25 minutes, depending on the complexity and length of the lecture and on the format you choose.

Transfer: Students in multinational classes will benefit from doing reports about their own countries on topics from the lectures. Students from the same country can work together to prepare the reports and present the information as a panel or assign one individual to present it. In either case, students should prepare brief notes to speak from rather than write out the full report. Students in homogeneous classes, such as those in EFL settings, will find class discussions more interesting and less duplicative of effort and information. Time: will vary depending on the activity chosen, class size, and number of different national groups.

Collaboration: Appoint one member of the group as a leader, one as a recorder, and one as a reporter (when appropriate). Establish realistic time limits for completing the activity. Allow enough time for sharing upon completion of the task. Each group should receive peer feedback especially for summary writing and essay question answer writing. If time is short, assign fewer questions per group for the discussion and essay question answer writing. Time: depends on which skill is being practiced and the number of questions assigned.

Pursuing the Topic: If your schedule and course design allow, you may want to use our suggestions for further study of the topic. We have tried to include suggestions for further listening, reading, and speaking, but not every topic lends itself easily to all three. The suggestions are obviously not exhaustive, but they may remind you of works that you find more suitable for use with your students. Or the students themselves can treat this activity as a research project in which they look for articles, stories, and books that they read and report to the class on. Students in an EFL setting, who will have difficulty finding informants for interviews, may be able to locate one American who would be willing to be interviewed by the whole class. Time: will vary according to the material and activities chosen.

Follow-up Activities: Keep all follow-up activities as brief as possible. Besides providing feedback, they are also meant to remind students of the purpose of the just-completed task and to provide closure before moving to the next activity. Time: 2–3 minutes.

Unit Quiz Preparation: Our experience is that students retain information better and do better on quizzes when they anticipate the questions that will be asked. Use this section to help students anticipate quiz questions by having them review their notes and then write practice short-answer and essay exam questions. To save class time, students can review their notes at home by looking at the information in terms of main ideas and details that support the main ideas within each major subtopic. In class, small groups should then be ready to write short-answer questions that focus more on the details of the lecture as well as essay exam questions that focus more on the main ideas, albeit with support from details.

Students may well benefit from a reminder about correct question form: *question word/auxiliary/subject/verb,* in most cases. You may also want to walk around and give some guidance as students work, especially in the first units, to make sure that students understand their task. It is probably advisable to tell them that the quiz you eventually give will not derive directly from their questions; at the same time, if their notes are accurate and well-organized, they will have asked many of the same questions that the authors provide in the unit quizzes. Use the follow-up as a chance for students to evaluate their comprehension/retention of the lecture. Discuss their short-answer questions; use the better ones as review. Discuss their essay questions; choose one or two for written follow-up if desired. Time: 8–10 minutes per chapter.

Unit Quizzes (in the *Tapescript and Answer Key*): The primary purposes of the quizzes are to build motivation to take good notes and to simulate a college experience. In a college class, students take notes that they later use to study from to prepare for tests. The time interval can be rather short, or it can be quite long—several weeks, for example.

We suggest giving a quiz on each unit. Assign point values to each question. Short-answer questions obviously earn fewer points than essay questions, and you may want to weight more difficult questions with additional points. On a 25-point scale, the short-answer questions could count a total of 10 points and the essay questions, if both are assigned, a total of 15 points.

We suggest that you let students know how much each question is worth and how much time they should devote to each portion of the quiz.

If the class has studied all three chapters in a unit, you will have to make a decision about the number of essay questions to require on the quiz. Depending on the level of your class and the class time you can allot to the quiz, you may choose only one of the two essay questions for each chapter or let students make their own choice.

Another decision is whether you want your students to study their notes outside class or whether they can use them during the quiz. There are good arguments on both sides of the decision, and the goals of your particular class will help you decide. Initially, you may want to let students use their notes so that the point of having complete, usable notes is made. Having students study their notes but not use them during the quiz, however, more closely duplicates the college experience. Teachers in academic preparation programs will probably want to give students this experience.

THE FACE OF THE PEOPLE

THE POPULATION 1

1. Prelistening Activities

A. Discussion

Discuss the following questions with your classmates:

- ○ Does this picture match your idea of the make-up of the United States population?

- ○ How many different races or ethnic groups are shown in the picture?

- ○ Are there more old people or young people?

- ○ Is the average age of the population in your country higher or lower than in the United States?

- ○ Why do you think so?

B. Vocabulary and Key Concepts

Read through the sentences, trying to imagine which words would fit in the blanks. Then listen to a dictation of the full sentences, and write the missing words in the blanks.

1. Most countries take a _____ every ten years or so in order to count the people and to know where they are living.

2. A country with a growing population is a country that is becoming

   more _____.

3. A person's _____ is partly determined by skin color and type of hair as well as other physical characteristics.

4. The majority of the U.S. population is of European

   _____.

5. The _____ _____ of a country's population gives information about where the people are living.

6. The total population of the United States is

_____ _____

_____ many different kinds of people.

7. In other words, the population _____ people
of different races and ages.

8. The average age of the U.S. population, which is a _____
large one, has been getting _____ higher recently.

9. _____ areas are more _____
populated than rural areas. That is, they have more people per square
mile.

10. The use of antibiotics has greatly _____ the

_____ _____

throughout much of the world.

11. A country whose _____

_____ is higher than its death rate will have

an _____ population.

12. On the average, women have a higher _____

_____ than men do.

Follow-up: Check the spelling of the dictated words with your teacher.
Discuss the meanings of these words and any other unfamiliar words in
the sentences.

C. Predictions

Using the photograph and the vocabulary exercise as a starting point,
write three questions that you think will be answered in the lecture.

Examples: ○   Is the number of minorities increasing or decreasing?
              ○   Why is the average age of the U.S. population increasing?

1. _____

_____

2. _____

_____

3. _____

_____

Follow-up: After you have written your questions, share them with your teacher and your classmates.

D. Notetaking Preparation

1. Number Notation

During today's talk you will need to write down many numbers. Some of these will be expressed as whole numbers, some as percentages, some as fractions, and some as ratios. Let's do a little practice before the lecture. Here are some examples: If you hear "thirty-seven million," you should write this _whole number_ as _37 mill._ If you hear "three fourths," you should write this _fraction_ as _3/4._ If you hear "one out of six," you should write this _ratio_ as _1:6._ If you hear "thirteen point four percent," you should write this _percentage_ as _13.4%._ Let's practice.

a. _____   **f.** _____

b. _____   **g.** _____

c. _____   **h.** _____

d. _____   **i.** _____

e. _____   **j.** _____

Follow-up: Check your answers with your teacher by saying each one as you write it on the board.

2. Rhetorical Cues

Lecturers usually use _rhetorical cues_ to help their listeners follow the lecture. A rhetorical cue is a word or even a sentence which lets us know that some important information is coming or that a new subtopic or point is being introduced. Look at these rhetorical cues, and decide in which order you will probably hear them in today's lecture. Order them from first (1) to fifth (5).

_____ **a.** Another way of looking at the population . . .

_____ **b.** Today we're going to talk about population . . .

_____ **c.** First of all, let's take a look . . .

_____ **d.** Now, to finish up . . .

_____ **e.** Before we finish today . . .

Follow-up: Discuss your answers as a class.

2. Listening

A. First Listening

Listen for general ideas. After a brief introduction, the lecturer lists his three subtopics. He then goes on to discuss each one individually. As you listen, write down the three major subtopics in the spaces labeled ST1, ST2, and ST3. Take down details you have time for, but make sure you take down the subtopics.

NOTES

Introduction:

ST1 _____

ST2 _____

Follow-up: Now check your major subtopics with your teacher.

B. Further Listening

While listening again, write down necessary relevant details below the main subtopic to which they belong. Remember to use proper number notation to save time.

Follow-up: Check your notes. If you missed important information or have doubts about your notes, 1) verify them by asking a classmate questions to fill the gaps in your notes or 2) listen to the lecture a third time. When verifying your notes with a classmate, do not show each other your notes; ask specific questions to get the information you need.

Examples: ○ In what regions do most people in the U.S. live?
○ What percentage of the population is black?
○ Did the lecturer say there were six million more women than men in the U.S. population?

This is also a good time to check to see if the lecturer answered your *Predictions* questions about the lecture.

3. Postlistening Activities

A. Accuracy Check

Listen to the following questions, and write *short answers*. Use your notes. You will hear each question one time only.

1. _____

2. _____

3. _____

4. _____

5. _____

6. _____

7. _____

8. _____

9. _____

10. _____

Follow-up: Check your answers with your teacher. If your score is less than 70%, you may need to listen to the lecture again or rewrite your notes so that you can understand and retrieve the information in them.

B. Oral Activities

1. Review

In pairs, use your notes to reproduce sections of the lecture. Student A will present the introduction and subtopic 1, including details, to Student B. Student B will present subtopics 2 and 3 with details to Student A. Check what you hear against your notes. If you don't understand or you disagree with what you hear, wait until your partner finishes. Then bring your notes into agreement by seeking clarification, as follows:

○ Excuse me. I didn't hear your percentage for Americans of Asian origin. Could you repeat it, please?

○ I don't think I agree with what you said about the five most populous states. I think the five most populous states are . . . .

○ I'm afraid my notes are different from yours . . . .

2. Transfer

If your class is multinational, prepare a short oral report about the population of your country, covering the points below. Work with the other students from your country.

If your classmates are all from your country, discuss the population of your country as a class. Discuss these points:

- ○ the size of the population and where it is distributed geographically

- ○ the most populous regions or cities

- ○ whether the population in your country is increasing or decreasing and why

C. Collaboration: Summary

In groups of three, with one member acting as secretary, write a one-paragraph summary of the lecture on population. Use the questions below to decide which information to include. Write the answers in complete sentences in paragraph form, but limit your summary to 125 words.

- ○ What is the present U.S. population?

- ○ What are the percentages of the different races that make up the U.S. population?

- ○ Which regions and states are the most populous? Is the population more rural or urban?

- ○ Why are there more women than men? How much higher is women's life expectancy than men's?

- ○ Is the average age of the population increasing or decreasing?

Follow-up: Exchange summaries with at least one other group. Check if the other group has summarized the lecture in a similar fashion.

D. Pursuing the Topic

The following are recommended for a closer look at the population of the United States:

Books/Periodicals

"How Old Is Old?" *USA Today* (Magazine), December 1992, p. 3.

A lot of the perceptions about the elderly are based on stereotypes and are inaccurate. These misperceptions are perpetuated by both young and old.

Randall, Teri. "Demographers Ponder the Aging of the Aged and Await Unprecedented Looming Elder Boom." *The Journal of the American Medical Association*, v. 269, May 12, 1993, pp. 2331–32.

Accompanied by other articles, this one takes a statistical yet clear look at the increase in average age of the U.S. population.

Any contemporary encyclopedia in English. Look up "United States," and find a section that interests you. For example, you could choose among population, rural and urban life, history, geography, and climate.

GENERAL PUTNAM

Immigrants arriving by ferry at Ellis Island around 1920.

Immigrants taking a mental health exam administered by public health doctor with the help of an interpreter.

IMMIGRATION: PAST AND PRESENT

2

1. Prelistening Activities

A. Discussion

Discuss the following questions with your classmates:

○ Do you think there is more or less immigration to the United States now than in the past?

○ Have the countries of origin of the immigrants changed over the years?

○ Do you think people's reasons for immigrating to the United States are the same today as they were in the past?

○ Have people from your country immigrated to the United States? If so, how many? Why?

B. Vocabulary and Key Concepts

Read through the sentences, trying to imagine which words would fit in the blanks. Then listen to a dictation of the full sentences, and write the missing words in the blanks.

1. Throughout history, people have moved, or

    _____, to new countries to live.

2. _____ _____ can take many forms: those which are characterized by a shortage of rain or

    food are called _____ and

    _____, respectively.

3. Sometimes people immigrate to a new country to escape political or

   religious _____ .

4. Rather than immigrants, the early _____ from

   Great Britain considered themselves _____ ;
   they had left home to settle new land for the mother country.

5. The so-called Great Immigration, which can be divided into three

   _____ , or time periods, began about 1830 and
   lasted till about 1930.

6. The Industrial Revolution, which began in the nineteenth century,

   caused _____ _____
   as machines replaced workers.

7. The _____ of farmland in Europe caused
   many people to immigrate to the United States, where farmland was
   more abundant.

8. Land in the United States was plentiful and available when the

   country was _____ westward. In fact, the U.S.

   government offered free public land to _____
   in 1862.

9. The _____ of the Irish potato crop in the
   middle of the nineteenth century caused widespread starvation.

10. The Great Depression of the 1930s and World War II contributed to

    the noticeable _____ in immigration after
    1930.

11. Although the U.S. government has _____ the
    number of immigrants ever since the Chinese Exclusion Act of 1882,

    _____ to the limit are sometimes made.

12. Exceptions to immigration laws have been made occasionally in cases

    where wars or other _____ displaced people
    from their own countries. Most recently, the U.S. government has felt

    a responsibility to accept _____ from Vietnam
    and Cuba, for example.

13. The U.S. immigration laws of today in general require that new immi-

grants have the _____ necessary to succeed in
the U.S. because industry no longer requires large numbers of

_____ workers.

Follow-up: Check the spelling of the dictated words with your teacher. Discuss the meanings of these words and any other unfamiliar words in the sentences.

C. Predictions

Using the photographs and the vocabulary exercise as a starting point, write three questions that you think will be answered in the lecture.

Examples: ○ Is immigration to the United States increasing or decreasing?
○ How many immigrants return to their countries of origin after a short time?

1. _____

_____

2. _____

_____

3. _____

_____

Follow-up: After you have written your questions, share them with your teacher and your classmates.

D. Notetaking Preparation

1. Dates: Teens and Tens

In dates, *teens* and *tens* (1815 and 1850, for example) are sometimes confused in listening. For teens, as in 1815, both syllables of *15* (FIF TEEN) are stressed, with heavier stress on the second syllable. For tens, as in 1850, only the first syllable is stressed (FIF ty). Write down the dates and phrases you hear. For a whole decade like the nineteen forties, write *the 1940s*.

a. _____   f. _____

b. _____   g. _____

c. _____   h. _____

d. _____   i. _____

e. _____   j. _____

Follow-up: Check your answers with your teacher by saying each one as you write it on the board.

2. *Language Conventions: Countries and Nationalities*

The lecturer uses the names of several countries as well as the names of the people who come from those countries. Check your knowledge of these names by completing the following chart in three minutes. A knowledge of the names of these countries and their people will help you recognize them when you hear them. Ask your instructor to pronounce the names of these countries and their people before you listen to the lecture. You will probably want to abbreviate some of these names as you take notes.

Country	People
_____	French
Germany	_____
_____	Scotch-Irish
_____	Britons; the British
_____	Danes
_____	Norwegians
_____	Swedes
Greece	_____
_____	Italians
_____	Spaniards
_____	Portuguese
China	_____
_____	Filipinos
_____	Mexicans
Korea	_____
the West Indies	_____
India	_____
_____	Russians
_____	Poles

Follow-up: After you check your answers with your teacher, answer these questions: Which of the above are Scandinavian countries? Which are Southern European countries? Which are Eastern European countries? Check your answers with your teacher.

2. Listening

A. First Listening

After a rather long introduction in which the lecturer discusses what immigration is, some general reasons that people immigrate, and the kinds of people who came to what is now the United States while it was still a colony of Great Britain, he goes on to discuss three main subtopics. In the first listening, make sure you get down the main subtopics; take down relevant details that you have time for, including those in the introduction.

NOTES

Introduction:

ST1 _____

ST2 _____

ST3 _____

Follow-up: Now check your major subtopics with your teacher.

B. Further Listening

While listening again, write down necessary relevant details below the main subtopic to which they belong. Remember to use proper number notation and abbreviations to save time.

Follow-up: Check your notes. If you missed important information or have doubts about your notes, 1) verify them by asking a classmate questions to fill the gaps in your notes or 2) listen to the lecture a third time. When verifying your notes with a classmate, do not show each other your notes; ask specific questions to get the information you need.

Examples: ❍ Could you please tell me what the lecturer said about the composition of the U.S. population in the Colonial Period?
❍ What was said about Ireland and the crop failure?

This is also a good time to check to see if the lecturer answered your *Predictions* questions about the lecture.

3. Postlistening Activities

A. Accuracy Check

Listen to the following questions, and write *short answers*. Use your notes. You will hear each question one time only.

1. _____

2. _____

3. _____

4. _____

5. _____

6. _____

7. _____

8. _____

9. _____

10. _____

Follow-up: Check your answers with your teacher. If your score is less than 70%, you may need to listen to the lecture again or rewrite your notes so that you can understand and retrieve the information in them.

B. Oral Activities

1. Review

In groups of four, practice giving sections of the lecture to each other. Take turns practicing different sections until everyone has had a chance to speak. Student A will give the introduction, Student B will give subtopic 1, and so on. Check what you hear against your notes. If you don't understand or you disagree with what you hear, wait until the speaker finishes. Then bring your notes into agreement by clarifying points of disagreement, as follows:

❍ Could you repeat what you said about the population during the Colonial Period?

❍ My notes are different from yours. You said . . . the famine was in England, but I think you're wrong. Let's see what the others have in their notes.

2. Transfer

Discuss with your teacher and classmates reasons why people either leave your country or come to your country. Do people leave your country for economic reasons? For educational reasons? Do they usually return home? Do people come to your country to work or to study? If so, who are these people? Do any of these people become citizens? How long do they stay in your country? What are some of the benefits of having immigrants in a country? What are some of the disadvantages?

C. Collaboration: Writing Answers to Essay Questions

On the quiz at the end of this unit, there will be short-answer questions and essay questions. You will answer the short-answer questions with a few words or a sentence or two. You will answer the essay questions with a complete English paragraph.

In groups of three or four, plan and write essay answers to the following questions on immigration. Appoint one member to write; all members will participate in planning and helping with the answer.

Use these guidelines:

1. Take the question and turn it into a general topic sentence to start your paragraph. For Question #1 below, you might begin: *Between 1830 and 1930, Europeans immigrated to the United States for a number of reasons.*

2. Choose specific relevant points from the lecture to support the topic sentence.

3. Make a brief outline of your answer so that when you write it you can concentrate on writing rather than remembering.

4. Write full sentences to develop your answer. (On a quiz, do not simply *list* points of support unless you run out of time.)

5. Write only the information that the question asks for. (If you do not know or are unsure of the answer to a quiz question, write a quick, brief answer to get some points, and concentrate on the other questions.)

6. Refer to *Writing Essay Questions* on p. 30 for information on what head-words such as *discuss* and *explain* require in the answer.

Questions:

1. Discuss the reasons why Europeans immigrated to the U.S. between 1830 and 1930.

2. Explain how immigration today is different from immigration to the U.S. in the past. Discuss the origin of immigrants and reasons for immigrating.

3. Describe the population of the U.S. during the Colonial Period. (Was it the same or different from now?)

Follow-up: Share your answers with at least one other group. Or share your answers orally as a class, and discuss the strengths in each answer.

D. Pursuing the Topic

The following are recommended for a closer look at immigration in the United States:

Books/Periodicals

Sowell, Thomas. *Ethnic America: A History*. New York: Basic Books, 1981.

Sowell discusses the contributions of different ethnic and racial groups in the United States.

Films/Videos

Avalon, Barry Levinson, director; 126 minutes, PG.

The film spans fifty years in the lives of a Russian immigrant family.

Malcolm X, Spike Lee, director; 201 minutes, PG-13.

Biographical film of a famous African American civil rights leader; the film shows the influences, including painful white influences, on the leader's life.

Interview

Interview someone whose parents or grandparents immigrated to the United States. Beforehand, prepare interview questions as a class to ask

○ where the person immigrated from

○ when and why the person immigrated

○ other questions your class is interested in

Write down the answers to the questions, and share the information with your classmates.

Variation: Invite an American to visit your class, and have the whole class interview him or her by using the questions you wrote.

AMERICANS AT WORK

3

1. Prelistening Activities

A. Discussion

Discuss the following questions with your classmates:

○ Of every 100 Americans, how many do you think work for the government?

○ How many work in manufacturing?

○ Is it common for U.S. women to work?

○ How seriously do Americans take their jobs?

○ How might the average U.S. worker differ from the average worker in your country?

B. Vocabulary and Key Concepts

Read through the sentences, trying to imagine which words would fit in the blanks. Then listen to a dictation of the full sentences, and write the missing words in the blanks.

1. The topic of work in the United States is an interesting one because

   the _____ do not always agree with popular general impressions about American workers.

2. Let's take a look at 100 _____ workers and see

   where they're _____.

3. _____ _____, then, include a wide variety of businesses that provide services rather than produce goods.

4. _____ trade involves purchases directly from the producer, while _____ trade is more familiar to us: purchases from stores, automobile dealerships, and so on.

5. Two smaller sectors include _____, along with banks and the stock market, and _____, which should make you think of gas and electricity.

6. Communication, of course, includes newspapers, magazines, and books as well as TV and radio _____.

7. Still others work in _____, and a smaller number works in agriculture, _____, and fishing.

8. Workers with a strong _____ _____ feel an obligation to work hard and take _____ in doing their jobs well.

9. According to _____, most Americans feel they should work harder.

10. The reason they give for not working harder is that they don't feel they will _____ from the work.

11. The solution suggested by at least one expert has two parts, both involving _____, or encouragement, to work harder.

Follow-up: Check the spelling of the dictated words with your teacher. Discuss the meanings of these words and any other unfamiliar words in the sentences.

C. Predictions

Using the photographs and the vocabulary exercise as a starting point, write three questions that you think will be answered in the lecture.

Examples: ○ Why do Americans feel they should work harder?
○ What percentage of American women work?

1. _____

_____

2. _____

_____

3. _____

_____

Follow-up: After you have written your questions, share them with your teacher and your classmates.

D. Notetaking Preparation

1. Abbreviations

To save time and get down more information when you listen to a lecture, it is helpful to abbreviate words. It is important to abbreviate them in a way that will allow you to remember what the full form is, of course. Another person's abbreviation may not help you remember. Practice abbreviating the following terms you will hear, but in a way so that you will know what each abbreviation stands for a few days or few weeks later. Look at the examples to see how some terms from the lecture have been abbreviated.

Examples: ○ computer programming and data processing: *comp. prog. & d. proc.*
 ○ statistics: *stats.*

Term	Abbreviation
a. manufacturing	_____
b. service industries	_____
c. workers	_____
d. wholesale and retail trade	_____
e. transportation, communication, and utilities	_____
f. Japan, Korea, and Germany	_____
g. decisions	_____
h. finance, insurance, and real estate	_____
i. community, social, and personal services	_____
j. technology	_____

Follow-up: With a partner, take turns covering up the left column. Looking at the right column, practice saying the terms that your abbreviations stand for. Your partner will check your accuracy.

2. Rhetorical Cues

Lecturers usually use *rhetorical cues* to help their listeners follow the lecture. A rhetorical cue is a word or even a sentence which lets us know that some important information is coming or that a new subtopic or point is being introduced. Look at these rhetorical cues, and decide in which order you will probably hear them in today's lecture. Order them from first (1) to fifth (5).

_____ **a.** Before I discuss the work ethic, I'd like to make a slight digression.

_____ **b.** To get you warmed up, let me give you a few questions to think about before I start the first point of our lecture today.

_____ **c.** Well, I see that our time is up.

_____ **d.** Now that we've taken care of that digression, let's talk about our last topic: the work ethic.

_____ **e.** Before we leave our first topic, let's check to make sure you have all the figures for the 76 workers in the service industries.

Follow-up: Discuss your answers as a class.

2. Listening

A. First Listening

Listen for general ideas. The lecturer gives a preview of the lecture by asking three questions in the introduction. He then goes on to discuss the first question at length. The second question is discussed so briefly that it is more of a digression than a subtopic. It is important to include it in your notes, however. The lecturer discusses the third question in some detail. As you listen, decide what the two main subtopics are, and write them down under ST1 and ST2. You might want to put large parentheses around the brief digression between the two subtopics. Take down details you have time for, but make sure you take down the subtopics.

NOTES

Introduction:

ST1 _____

(Digression)

ST2 _____

Follow-up: Now check your major subtopics with your teacher.

B. Further Listening

While listening again, write down necessary relevant details below the main subtopics to which they belong. Remember to use proper number notation and abbreviations to save time.

Follow-up: Check your notes. If you missed important information or have doubts about your notes, 1) verify them by asking a classmate questions to fill the gaps in your notes or 2) listen to the lecture a third time. When verifying your notes with a classmate, do not show each other your notes; ask specific questions to get the information you need.

Examples: ○   Did you take down what the lecturer said about the difference between the service industries and manufacturing?

○ What is the difference between retail and wholesale trade?

○ What does "work ethic" mean?

This is also a good time to check to see if the lecturer answered your *Predictions* questions about the lecture.

3. Postlistening Activities

A. Accuracy Check

Listen to the following questions, and write *short answers*. Use your notes. You will hear each question one time only.

1. _____

2. _____

3. _____

4. _____

5. _____

6. _____

7. _____

8. _____

9. _____

10. _____

Follow-up: Check your answers with your teacher. If your score is less than 70%, you may need to listen to the lecture again or rewrite your notes so that you can understand and retrieve the information in them.

B. Oral Activities

1. Review

In pairs, use your notes to reproduce sections of the lecture. Student A will present the introduction and subtopic 1, including details, to Student B. Student B will present subtopic 2 with details to Student A. Check what you hear against your notes. If you don't understand or you disagree with what you hear, wait until your partner finishes. Then bring your notes into agreement by seeking clarification, as follows:

○ Could you repeat what you said about the number of workers in service industries?

○ I'm sorry. I don't believe I understood what you said about women in the U.S. labor force.

2. Transfer

If your class is multinational, prepare a short oral report about work in your country, covering the points below. Work with the other students from your country.

If your classmates are all from your country, discuss work in your country as a class. Discuss these points:

○ what most people do

○ how important manufacturing and agriculture are to the economy

○ what the role of women is in the work force

○ how strong you feel your country's work ethic is

C. Collaboration: Discussion

Discuss the questions in small groups. Appoint one person to report your group's opinions to the class.

1. What are the benefits of a strong work ethic? What are some possible negative effects?
2. Do you agree that incentives like more money for harder work and more control over their work would encourage U.S. workers to work harder? Why or why not?
3. Japanese workers, who do not receive higher wages than U.S. workers, have a reputation for working very hard. What might explain the strong Japanese work ethic?
4. Compare the U.S. work ethic as described in the lecture to the work ethic in your country.

D. Pursuing the Topic

The following are recommended for a closer look at work in the United States:

Books/Periodicals

Saltzman, Amy. "Working It Out." *U.S. News & World Report*, February 17, 1992, p. 15.

This brief article discusses the work ethic of U.S employees.

Films/Videos

American Dream, Barbara Kopple, director; 100 minutes, no rating.

The film shows the attempts of workers at a huge meat-packing plant to negotiate salaries with the help of their union.

Interview

Interview an American who has worked at a job for at least five years. Beforehand, prepare interview questions as a class to ask

○ where the person works

○ how long he or she has worked there

○ how he or she feels about the job

○ what the person's favorite and least favorite parts of the job are

○ whether the person feels that Americans work hard

○ other questions your class is interested in

Write down the answers to the questions, and share the information with your classmates.

Variation: Invite an American to visit your class, and have the whole class interview him or her by using the questions you wrote.

UNIT QUIZ DIRECTIONS

Now that you have completed from one to three chapters in this unit, your teacher may want you to take a quiz on the chapter(s). Your teacher will tell you whether or not you can use your notes to answer the questions on the quiz. If you can use your notes, review them before taking the quiz so that you can anticipate the questions and know where to find the answers. If you cannot use your notes on the quiz, *study them carefully before you take the quiz*, concentrating on organizing the information into main ideas and details that support these main ideas.

Work in small groups to help each other anticipate the questions your teacher will ask. Before breaking up into groups, review your notes and highlight important, noteworthy points. After reviewing your notes, break up into groups. Discuss and write specific short-answer questions and more general essay questions. Follow these guidelines in writing the questions:

Writing Short-Answer Questions

Short-answer questions . . .

○ should be specific, easy to answer in a few words or two sentences at most.

○ should be clearly stated so that it is obvious what answer is wanted.

○ should ask for facts, not opinions or information outside the lecture.

Exercise 1

Judge these questions by the above criteria. Mark each question + if it is good and – if it is bad. Discuss reasons for your choices, citing the criteria above.

_____ 1. Talk about the work ethic.

_____ 2. Does your country have a work ethic?

_____ 3. What is the basic difference between the service industries and manufacturing?

_____ 4. What percentage of U.S. women work?

_____ 5. Analyze the conflict that exists in the U.S. work ethic.

Writing Essay Questions

Essay questions...

○ are usually in the form of a statement.

○ are more general and require at least a paragraph—that is, several sentences—to answer fully.

○ usually begin with a headword such as *discuss, describe, explain, compare and contrast, list, analyze,* or *summarize.* These headwords explain the writer's purpose in answering the question:

1. to give all sides of the topic (discuss)

2. to give all the important details of something (describe)

3. to make something clear by giving reasons or by explaining how to do it (explain)

4. to write the similarities and differences (compare and contrast)

5. to name the parts of something, one by one (list)

6. to break something into its logical parts in order to explain it (analyze)

7. to write something in a shorter form, giving the main ideas and omitting the details (summarize)

Exercise 2

Judge these questions by the above characteristics. Mark each question + if it is good and – if it is bad. Discuss reasons for your choices, citing the characteristics above.

_____ 1. Discuss the U.S. work ethic, its problems, and possible solutions.

_____ 2. List the percentage of U.S. women who work.

_____ 3. Contrast the service industries with the manufacturing sector of the U.S. economy in terms of products and number of people employed.

_____ 4. Discuss the sectors of the U.S. economy, including the number of workers in each.

Write your group's questions on the following pages.

Unit Quiz Preparation

Assign one group member to write down the questions; all members will help plan and compose the questions. For the lecture on population, write five short-answer questions that can be answered with a few words or a maximum of two sentences.

1. _____

   _____

2. _____

   _____

3. _____

   _____

4. _____

   _____

5. _____

   _____

Follow-up: Write your questions on the board to discuss as a class.

Written follow-up: Prepare for the quiz by writing answers to the questions your class has proposed. You have abbreviations in your notes, but do not use abbreviations other than standard ones like *U.S.* in your answers.

Unit Quiz Preparation

Assign one group member to write down the questions; all members will help plan and compose the questions. For the lecture on immigration, write three to five short-answer questions that can be answered with a few words or sentences. In addition, write two essay questions; word the questions so that they can easily be turned into topic sentences.

Short-Answer Questions

1. _____

   _____

2. _____

   _____

3. _____

   _____

4. _____

   _____

5. _____

   _____

Essay Questions

1. _____

   _____

2. _____

   _____

Follow-up: Write your questions on the board to discuss as a class.

Written follow-up: Prepare for the quiz by writing answers to the questions your class has proposed. You have abbreviations in your notes, but do not use abbreviations other than standard ones like *U.S.* in your answers.

Unit Quiz Preparation

Assign one group member to write down the questions; all members will help plan and compose the questions. For the lecture on work, write three to five short-answer questions that can be answered with a few words or sentences. In addition, write two essay questions; word the questions so that they can easily be turned into topic sentences.

Short-Answer Questions

1. _____

   _____

2. _____

   _____

3. _____

   _____

4. _____

   _____

5. _____

   _____

Essay Questions

1. _____

   _____

2. _____

   _____

Follow-up: Write your questions on the board to discuss as a class.

Written follow-up: Prepare for the quiz by writing answers to the questions your class has proposed. You have abbreviations in your notes, but do not use abbreviations other than standard ones like *U.S.* in your answers.

THE AMERICAN CHARACTER

Ricky, Ozzie, David, and
Harriet Nelson from the
popular TV show *Ozzie
and Harriet* (ca. 1949)

THE AMERICAN FAMILY

1. Prelistening Activities

A. Discussion

Discuss the following questions with your classmates:

○ Does the family in this picture represent your idea of today's typical American family? Why or why not?

○ Are single-parent families common in your country?

○ Is it common for parents in your country to leave children in day care while they work?

○ Who takes care of the children when parents are not home?

B. Vocabulary and Key Concepts

Read through the sentences, trying to imagine which words would fit in the blanks. Then listen to a dictation of the full sentences, and write the missing words in the blanks.

1. A hundred years ago, one heard the same comments about the family that one hears today—in short, that the American family is

   _____.

2. Proof of this disintegration included evidence that women were not

   completely content with their _____

   _____.

3. To the contrary, the very _____ of the family

   has changed _____ in the last 50 years.

4. To be sure, the family is a very _____

_____ for what is happening in the society.

5. Demographically, the _____

_____ of the family was the traditional one.

6. The country idealized the family in these years: there was a

_____ to the family and a

_____ for it.

7. Three characteristics stand out in this period:

_____ to social norms, greater male domina-

tion of the family, and clearcut _____ roles.

8. These decades were characterized by a _____
of conformity to social norms and included the sexual revolution and

the women's _____ movement.

9. Another important movement was the drive for self-expression and

_____-_____.

10. The new configuration of the family had to include families of

_____ _____, with or
without children.

11. The number of single-parent households _____,

and the number of unmarried couples _____.

12. Most experts admit that children paid a high price for the social
changes, including spending long days in

_____ _____ and

living with _____.

13. There is an attempt to _____ work with family
obligations, and concern seems to be shifting from

_____ to the new familism.

14. Places of work may offer more _____ working

hours and _____-_____
day care.

15. For its part, the government could _____

parental leave and family _____.

Follow-up: Check the spelling of the dictated words with your teacher. Discuss the meanings of these words and any other unfamiliar words in the sentences.

C. Predictions

Using the photograph and the vocabulary exercise as a starting point, write three questions that you think will be answered in the lecture.

Examples: ○ How big are American families compared to those in other parts of the world?
○ Does a divorced mother sometimes move back with her parents?

1. _____

_____

2. _____

_____

3. _____

_____

Follow-up: After you have written your questions, share them with your teacher and your classmates.

D. Notetaking Preparation

1. Key Words: Content Words

A good notetaker knows that it is neither efficient nor necessary to take down a lecture word for word. A good notetaker listens for relevant information and then uses key words to take down only the essential information. A good way to pick key words is to concentrate on the *content words* you hear: nouns, verbs, adjectives, and adverbs. (Auxiliaries, the verb *to be*, pronouns, and prepositions are *structure words*, words that receive less stress when spoken. They are less important in your notes, too.)

Practice reducing information to key words by using the sentences from Vocabulary and Key Concepts. Do sentences 5, 7, 8, 11, and 12. Sentence 2 is done for you.

2. <u>Proof of disintegration: women not content with domestic role.</u>

_____

5. _____

_____

7. _____

_____

8. _____

_____

11. _____

_____

12. _____

_____

Follow-up: With a partner, test your key words by trying to recall all the information in the sentences from what you wrote. Your partner will check to see if you can recall the *message*, not necessarily the exact words of the original sentences. Then change roles and test your partner's key words in the same way.

2. Rhetorical Cues

Lecturers usually use *rhetorical cues* to help their listeners follow the lecture. A rhetorical cue is a word or even a sentence which lets us know that some important information is coming or that a new subtopic or point is being introduced. Look at these rhetorical cues, and decide in which order you will probably hear them in today's lecture. Order them from first (1) to fifth (5).

_____ **a.** Well, let's proceed in chronological order and start with the traditional familism.

_____ **b.** The third period, the new familism, is harder to see because we are living in this period now.

_____ **c.** The second period, the period of individualism, saw three important social and political movements.

_____ **d.** To make this point clearer, we'll take a look at how the American family has changed in the last 50 years by looking at three different time periods.

_____ **e.** Since individualism is so often mentioned in our discussion of U.S. culture and people, I should make a little detour before we discuss it.

Follow-up: Discuss your answers as a class.

2. Listening

A. First Listening

Listen for general ideas. The lecturer looks at changes in the family over the last 50 years and divides the changes into three different periods, each with its own label. For each period, the lecturer looks at cultural, economic, and demographic aspects of the family. As you listen, decide what the three different periods are, and write them under ST1, ST2, and ST3. Take down details you have time for, but make sure you take down the subtopics.

NOTES

Introduction:

ST1 _____

ST2  _____

ST3 _____

Follow-up: Now check your major subtopics with your teacher.

B. Further Listening

While listening again, write down necessary relevant details below the main subtopic to which they belong. Remember to use key words to save time.

Follow-up: Check your notes. If you missed important information or have doubts about your notes, 1) verify them by asking a classmate questions to fill the gaps in your notes or 2) listen to the lecture a third time. When verifying your notes with a classmate, do not show each other your notes; ask specific questions to get the information you need.

Examples:
- Do you have any idea what *domestic* means?
- Did you understand the explanation of *individualism*?
- How many different movements were discussed for the second period?

This is also a good time to check to see if the lecturer answered your *Predictions* questions about the lecture.

3. Postlistening Activities

A. Accuracy Check

Listen to the following questions, and write *short answers*. Use your notes. You will hear each question one time only.

1. _____
2. _____
3. _____
4. _____
5. _____
6. _____
7. _____
8. _____
9. _____
10. _____

Follow-up: Check your answers with your teacher. If your score is less than 70%, you may need to listen to the lecture again or rewrite your notes so that you can understand and retrieve the information in them.

B. Oral Activities

1. Review

In groups of three, use your notes to reproduce sections of the lecture. Each member of your group should bring up a point from the introduction that he or she finds interesting. Then Student A will present the information in subtopic 1, Student B the information in subtopic 2, and Student C the information in subtopic 3. If you don't understand or you disagree with what you hear, wait until your classmate finishes. Then bring your notes into agreement by seeking clarification, as follows:

○ Would you mind repeating what you said about the sexual revolution? I didn't catch it.

○ I don't think my notes agree with yours on the matter of cultural developments during the second period. In my notes, I wrote that. . . .

2. Transfer

If your class is multinational, prepare a short oral report about the family in your country, covering the points below. Work with the other students from your country.

If your classmates are all from your country, discuss the family in your country as a class. Discuss these points:

○ Is there a predominant family configuration in your country?

○ Has it changed in the last 50 years?

○ What effects have economic, demographic, and cultural changes had on the family in your country?

C. Collaboration: Summary

Work with a partner, and use your notes to write a summary of the lecture in 125 words or less. Answer this question for your first main idea sentence: *Has the U.S. family changed a little or a lot in the last 50 years*? Then characterize each of the three periods by choosing relevant information about demographic, cultural, and economic points.

Follow-up: Share your summary with at least one other pair. Find something you like in each summary that you read. Alternatively, your teacher may ask for volunteers to read their summaries to the class.

D. Pursuing the Topic

The following are recommended for a closer look at the American family:

Books/Periodicals

Chollar, Susan. "Happy Families: Who Says They All Have to Be Alike?" *American Health*, July–August 1993, pp. 52–57.

Chollar discusses a variety of successful family configurations.

Etzioni, Amitai. "Children of the Universe." *UTNE Reader*, May/June 1993, pp. 52–61.

> *Etzioni discusses the roles of U.S. parents and government in raising children.*

Kimmel, Michael. "What do Men Want?" *Harvard Business Review*, December 1993, pp. 50–63.

> *Changing economics force American men to redefine themselves, but U.S. companies aren't keeping up to allow men to take on their new roles.*

Films/Videos

Mrs. Doubtfire, Chris Columbus, director; 119 minutes, PG-13.

> *This comedy shows the extremes to which a father will go to be near his children after their mother divorces him.*

Kramer vs. Kramer, Robert Benton, director; 105 minutes.

> *A serious film that shows the break-up of a marriage and investigates the issue of child custody in such cases.*

RELIGION

1. Prelistening Activities

A. Discussion

Discuss the following questions with your classmates:

○ Where do you think the children in the picture are?

○ What are the children doing?

○ What do you think the expression "freedom of religion" means?

○ Are there many different religions in your country?

B. Vocabulary and Key Concepts

Read through the sentences, trying to imagine which words would fit in the blanks. Then listen to a dictation of the full sentences, and write the missing words in the blanks.

1. The single largest religious group consists of _____,

   who are found in more than 1,200 _____.

2. The number of Americans belonging to churches or other religious organizations is surprisingly high compared to other

   _____ nations.

3. This is not to suggest that religious _____ are not important in these other nations.

4. Freedom of worship is _____ by the First Amendment to the Constitution.

5. The First Amendment also _____ the separation of church and state.

6. The importance of religion in American history should not be

   _____.

7. I'd like to talk about the increasing _____

   religion has _____ in fairly recent history.

8. Religion had seemed to be in _____, but there

   was a religious _____ in the 1970s that
   surprised many people.

9. The religious revival was _____ in nature and,
   at first, largely confined to issues in the private sphere of life.

10. These issues, however, were very _____ in

    nature and became quite _____ in a short
    time.

11. Perhaps the "rise of the religious right" is a temporary

    _____ in American life.

12. Some people predict that American society will become increasingly

    _____ and less religious in the future; others

    predict a more _____ political atmosphere
    based on conservative religious belief.

Follow-up: Check the spelling of the dictated words with your teacher.
Discuss the meanings of these words and any other unfamiliar words in
the sentences.

C. Predictions

Using the photograph and the vocabulary exercise as a starting point,
write three questions that you think will be answered in the lecture.

Example: ○   What were the controversial issues that were involved in
               the religious revival in the 1970s?

1. _____

   _____

2. _____

   _____

3. _____

   _____

Follow-up: After you have written your questions, share them with
your teacher and your classmates.

D. Notetaking Preparation

1. Commonly Used Symbols and Abbreviations

To save time while taking notes, it is useful to use symbols and abbreviations. You may want to develop some of your own for words and phrases that you often hear. However, there are many that are commonly used that you may find very helpful. The following are some of these commonly used symbols and abbreviations. Put a check next to the ones that are new to you and that you think might be helpful in your notetaking. Refer back to this page from time to time to see if you are using all the symbols and short abbreviations that would be useful in your notetaking.

Symbols	
+	and, plus
&	and
−	less, minus
=	equals, is the same as, consists of
≠	does not equal, is different from
>	is greater than, is more than
<	is less than
—>	causes, results in, leads to
+>	does not cause, does not result in, does not lead to
<—	is caused by, results from
<+	is not caused by, does not result from
∴	therefore
∵	because, because of
↗	rises, increases
↘	goes down, decreases
'	minute, feet (e.g., 3' = 3 feet)
"	inches *or* ditto marks (repeat the word immediately above)
°	degrees
%	percent, percentage
$	dollar, money

Abbreviations (first six from Latin)

e.g.	for example
i.e.	that is
etc.	et cetera
cf.	compare
c.	about/approximately
ca.	about/approximately
w/	with
w/o	without

Listen to and take notes on the following sentences, which contain information taken from several lectures for which you could use some of the symbols and abbreviations above. Try to take down *content words*, abbreviate as many of these content words as possible, and use your notetaking symbols and abbreviations.

(a–c from lecture on population)

a. _____

b. _____

c. _____

(d–e from lecture on immigration)

d. _____

e. _____

(f–g from lecture on American family)

f. _____

g. _____

Follow-up: 1. Compare your notes with your classmates'. Reconstruct the full message of what you heard from your notes. Then compare your reconstructions with the actual information you listened to. 2. When you finish taking notes on today's lecture on religion, look at your notes and see if there were places that you missed where you could have used a symbol such as < or a short abbreviation such as w/o to save time.

2. Rhetorical Cues

Read the following sentences, which contain rhetorical cues to help you follow the organization of the lecture. Decide in which order you will probably hear them. Number them from first (1) to fifth (5).

_____ **a.** Let's consider the first way America differs from these other modernized nations.

_____ **b.** Finally, let's take a closer look at this rise in the influence of religion on American political life.

_____ **c.** There are two ways that religion in the United States differs from religion in other modernized nations.

_____ **d.** However, there is another somewhat contradictory difference that we should also consider.

_____ **e.** However, whether this group will be able to influence political life for a long time cannot be known.

Follow-up: Discuss your answers as a class.

2. Listening

A. First Listening

In the introduction the lecturer discusses the reasons for the great number of churches in the United States. At the end of the introduction he mentions the three subtopics he will go on to develop. Take down details you have time for, but be sure to take down the subtopics.

NOTES

Introduction:

ST1 _____

ST2 _____

ST3 _____

Conclusion:

Follow-up: Check your major subtopics with your teacher before you listen to the lecture for the second time.

B. Further Listening

While listening again, write down necessary relevant details below the main subtopic to which they belong. Remember to use symbols and abbreviations to save time.

Follow-up: Check your notes. If you missed important information or have doubts about your notes, 1) verify them by asking a classmate questions to fill the gaps in your notes or 2) listen to the lecture a third time. When verifying your notes with a classmate, do not show each other your notes; ask specific questions to get the information you need.

Examples:
- Do you remember which is the second largest religious group in America?
- What did the lecturer say about the First Amendment?
- What does "religious right" mean?
- Which people were surprised by the religious revival?

This is also a good time to check to see if the lecturer answered your *Predictions* questions about the lecture.

3. Postlistening Activities

A. Accuracy Check

Listen to the following questions, and write *short answers*. You will hear each question one time only.

1. _____

2. _____

3. _____

4. _____

5. _____

6. _____

7. _____

8. _____

9. _____

10. _____

Follow-up: Check your answers with your teacher. If your score is less than 70%, you may need to listen to the lecture again or rewrite your notes so that you can understand and retrieve the information in them.

B. Oral Activities

1. Review

In pairs, use your notes to reproduce sections of the lecture. Student A will present the introduction and subtopic 1, including details, to Student B. Then Student B will present subtopics 2 and 3 with details to Student A. Check what you hear against your notes. If you don't understand or you disagree with what you hear, wait until your partner finishes. Then bring your notes into agreement by seeking clarification, as follows:

○ Excuse me, what did you say about the television and film media?

○ I don't think your numbers are correct.

○ Could you repeat what you said about the future role of religion in America?

2. Transfer

Discuss these questions with a partner or in small groups if you and your classmates come from different countries. If not, discuss them with your teacher and classmates.

○ What are the major religious groups in your country?

○ What is the relationship between the government and religion in your country?

○ Do you think religion is becoming more or less important in your country? Explain.

C. Collaboration: Writing Answers to Essay Questions

To help you prepare for the essay questions in the Unit Quiz at the end of this unit, in groups of three or four, plan and write essay answers to the following questions on religion in the U.S. Appoint one member of the group to do the actual writing; all members of the group should participate in planning and helping with the answers. At this point, you should refer to the guidelines in Unit 1, Chapter 2, p. 18. Review the guidelines before you begin to write essay answers.

Questions:

1. Contrast religion in the United States with religion in other modernized European countries.

2. Describe the conflict between the government and the religious right on the issues of legalized abortion and prayer in schools.

Follow-up: Share your answers with at least one other group. Or share your answers orally as a class, and discuss the strengths in each answer.

D. Pursuing the Topic

The following are recommended for a closer look at religion in the United States:

Books/Periodicals

Any contemporary encyclopedia in English. Look up the names of various religious minorities in the United States, such as "Mormons," "Seventh-Day Adventists," or "Amish." Read to learn about their historical background, their major beliefs, and any problems they have had as a religious minority.

Films/Videos

Witness, Peter Weir, director; 112 minutes, R.

> *This film depicts the life of the Amish in the United States: their commitment to non-violence and the resulting culture clash when one of them accidentally witnesses a brutal murder.*

Interview

Interview an American about his or her views on religion in America. Beforehand, prepare interview questions as a class to ask on

○ religious background

○ role of religion in his or her life

○ his or her opinion about freedom of religion, the separation of church and state, prayer in public schools, and the relationship between politics and religion

○ any other questions your class is interested in

Write down your answers to the questions, and share the information with your classmates.

Variation: Invite an American to visit your class, and have the whole class interview him or her, using the questions you wrote.

PASSAGES: BIRTH, MARRIAGE, AND DEATH

1. Prelistening Activities

A. Discussion

Discuss the following questions with your classmates:

○ What event does this picture represent?

○ Does this picture remind you of the same event in your country?

○ What other major life events do most people experience?

B. Vocabulary and Key Concepts

Read through the sentences, trying to imagine which words would fit in the blanks. Then listen to a dictation of the full sentences, and write the missing words in the blanks.

1. Customs and traditions are often _____ to

   foreigners, partly because the customs are so _____
   that people accept them without ever thinking about them.

2. The birth of a baby is a _____ occasion in any

   family and is _____ in some way.

3. The baby _____ is given by a close friend or

   relative of the _____ mother.

4. The _____ - _____ -

   _____ is often invited to someone's home on

   some _____ so that she can be surprised.

5. Gifts may be small ones, depending on the financial situation of the

   _____, but there is always a very emotional

   _____ of good wishes for the coming baby.

6. Through advice and _____

   _____ _____,

   the expectant mother is _____ about the
   desirability of her situation.

7. In the past men were _____ from the

   _____ room, but today many men are with
   their wives to "coach" them through the birth.

8. Christians usually have a religious service, called a

   _____, for the new baby.

9. Some customs are generally _____ concerning

   _____, the engagement period, and the
   wedding ceremony.

10. Since priests, rabbis, and ministers are all legally

    _____ to marry couples, it is not necessary to

    have both a _____ and a religious ceremony.

11. Some customs about the _____ and

    _____ are rather _____
    in nature.

12. At the time of death, one decision is whether the funeral will be held
    in a church or in a funeral home; another decision is whether the

    body will be _____ or buried in a cemetery.

13. The family may choose to have a _____
    service instead of a funeral. In either case, the family may hold a

    _____, where the body of the deceased is
    displayed in its casket.

14. At a funeral, a _____ is usually given by

    someone close to the _____ person.

15. Those who want to express their _____

usually send a sympathy card to the _____
family.

Follow-up: Check the spelling of the dictated words with your teacher. Discuss the meanings of these words and any other unfamiliar words in the sentences.

C. Predictions

Using the photograph and the vocabulary exercise as a starting point, write three questions that you think will be answered in the lecture.

Examples: ○ Must a child's baptism take place in the same church that the parents were married in?
○ Why are dead bodies displayed in a casket before the funeral?

1. _____

_____

2. _____

_____

3. _____

_____

Follow-up: After you have written your questions, share them with your teacher and your classmates.

D. Notetaking Preparation

1. Key Words: Listening

We have already talked about using key words to save time and take good notes. Think of key words as a *telegram*, that is, the basic information in reduced form. Practice reducing the following sentences you will hear to key words. You will hear each sentence twice. Listen, decide on the key words, and write them in the space below. For example, as you listen to the first sentence, see how the author has used key words to reduce the information.

a. ethnic groups follow old customs, but *still* general culture in U.S.

b. _____

c. _____

d. _____

e. _____

Note: The notetaker here not only reduced the number of words in the sentence greatly but also reworded it somewhat. Can *you* recreate the message of the sentence from these notes? Or would your notes look different?

Follow-up: Use your key words to reproduce the messages you heard. Add any words necessary to make your sentences clear and grammatical. Work with a partner, or check your answers as a class.

2. Adverbs as Content Words

Since adverbs are content words, it is important to understand them and to get them down in your notes. Read these sentences from the lecture, focusing on the italicized adverbs. Discuss the difference in meaning, if any, when you substitute the adverb in parentheses.

a. *Almost always* a baby shower is arranged in secret so as to be a complete surprise to the mother-to-be. (Occasionally)

b. *Usually* she is invited to someone's home on one pretext or another. (Ordinarily)

c. There is *always* a very emotional outpouring of good wishes. (often)

d. Men *almost never* participate in these events. (seldom)

e. In the past, when births mainly took place at home, it was a *strictly* female event. (mainly)

f. For Christians, this service is *ordinarily* called a baptism. (sometimes)

g. It is very hard to generalize, but there are some customs that are *quite generally* observed. (traditionally)

2. Listening

A. First Listening

The lecturer begins his talk with a discussion of cultural traditions in general and of how the United States is somewhat different from many countries. He then announces his subtopics: birth, marriage, and death. Since you already know the subtopics, you will have time to write down some main and secondary ideas of support in the first listening. Use key words and structure your notes.

NOTES

Introduction:

ST1 _____

ST2 _____

ST3 _____

B. Further Listening

While listening again, write down necessary relevant details below the main subtopic to which they belong. Remember to use content words as key words to save time.

Follow-up: Check your notes. If you missed important information or have doubts about your notes, 1) verify them by asking a classmate questions to fill the gaps in your notes or 2) listen to the lecture a third time. When verifying your notes with a classmate, do not show each other your notes; ask specific questions to get the information you need.

Examples: ○ Can you explain what a baby shower is?
                 ○ What was said about marriage superstitions?
                 ○ What's the difference between a funeral and a memorial service?

This is also a good time to check to see if the lecturer answered your *Predictions* questions about the lecture.

3. Postlistening Activities

A. Accuracy Check

Listen to the following questions, and write *short answers*. Use your notes. You will hear each question one time only.

1. _____

2. _____

3. _____

4. _____

5. _____

6. _____

7. _____

8. _____

9. _____

10. _____

Follow-up: Check your answers with your teacher. If your score is less than 70%, you may need to listen to the lecture again or rewrite your notes so that you can understand and retrieve the information in them.

B. Oral Activities

1. Review

In pairs, use your notes to reproduce sections of the lecture. Student A will present the introduction and subtopic 1, including details, to Student B. Student B will present subtopics 2 and 3 with details to Student A. Check what you hear against your notes. If you don't understand or you disagree with what you hear, wait until your partner finishes. Then bring your notes into agreement by seeking clarification, as follows:

○ My notes are a little different from yours. I don't believe men are allowed to come to baby showers.

○ Excuse me. I didn't catch what you said about the tradition of what brides wear or carry at their weddings.

2. Transfer

Choose *one* of the major subtopics (birth, marriage, or death) and carefully describe your customs that differ from those in the United States. Your teacher may ask you to present your report orally to a small group or the whole class, or to write a paragraph to hand in.

C. Collaboration: Discussion

Discuss the questions below in small groups. Appoint one person to report your group's opinions to the class.

1. Is it surprising that people in the United States, with its great racial and ethnic diversity, celebrate birth, marriage, and death in similar ways? Why or why not?

2. Death is a topic that is very difficult for most Americans to talk about. What reasons might there be for their avoidance of the topic of death?

3. The lecturer mentioned that men almost never participate in baby showers but that husbands more and more frequently accompany their wives in the delivery room when the baby is born. Why would a shower be a strictly female event while the husband can attend his child's birth?

4. The lecturer discussed superstitions connected to weddings, specifically that a groom should not see the bride in her wedding dress before the ceremony. What reason might there be for this superstition? Does your culture have superstitions connected to weddings? Superstitions about births and deaths? What are they?

D. Pursuing the Topic

The following are recommended for a closer look at life passages in the United States:

Books/Periodicals

Kübler-Ross, Elisabeth. *On Death and Dying.* New York: Macmillan, 1969.

The author discusses terminal illness, dying, and how those involved can deal with these issues.

Films/Videos

Father of the Bride, Charles Shyer, director; 114 minutes, PG.

The comedy depicts a father's reaction to his daughter's falling in love, getting engaged, and finally getting married.

Steel Magnolias, Herbert Ross, director; 118 minutes, PG.

A sentimental look at marriage, motherhood, and the lives of women in a small Louisiana town.

UNIT QUIZ DIRECTIONS

Now that you have completed from one to three chapters in this unit, your teacher may want you to take a quiz on the chapter(s). Your teacher will tell you whether or not you can use your notes to answer the questions on the quiz. If you can use your notes, review them before taking the quiz so that you can anticipate the questions and know where to find the answers. If you cannot use your notes on the quiz, *study them carefully before you take the quiz*, concentrating on organizing the information into main ideas and details that support these main ideas.

Work in small groups to help each other anticipate the questions your teacher will ask. Before breaking up into groups, review your notes and highlight important, noteworthy points. After reviewing your notes, break up into groups. Discuss and write specific short-answer questions and more general essay questions. (For guidelines in writing questions, see the Unit Quiz Directions at the end of Unit 1.)

Write your group's questions on the following pages.

Unit Quiz Preparation

Assign one group member to write down the questions; all members will help plan and compose the questions. For the lecture on the family, write five short-answer questions that can be answered with a few words or sentences. In addition, write two essay questions; word the essay questions so that they can easily be turned into topic sentences.

Short-Answer Questions

1. _____

   _____

2. _____

   _____

3. _____

   _____

4. _____

   _____

5. _____

   _____

Essay Questions

1. _____

   _____

2. _____

   _____

Follow-up: Write your questions on the board to discuss as a class.

Written follow-up: Prepare for the quiz by writing answers to the questions your class has proposed. You have abbreviations in your notes, but do not use abbreviations other than standard ones like *U.S.* in your answers.

Unit Quiz Preparation

Assign one group member to write down the questions; all members will help plan and compose the questions. For the lecture on religion, write three to five short-answer questions that can be answered with a few words or a maximum of two sentences. In addition, write two essay questions; word the essay questions so that they can easily be turned into topic sentences.

Short-Answer Questions

1. _____

   _____

2. _____

   _____

3. _____

   _____

4. _____

   _____

5. _____

   _____

Essay Questions

1. _____

   _____

2. _____

   _____

Follow-up: Write your questions on the board to discuss as a class.

Written follow-up: Prepare for the quiz by writing answers to the questions your class has proposed. You may have abbreviations in your notes, but do not use abbreviations other than standard ones like *U.S.* in your answers.

Unit Quiz Preparation

UNIT 2: CHAPTER 6

Assign one group member to write down the questions; all members will help plan and compose the questions. For the lecture on passages, write five short-answer questions that can be answered with a few words or sentences. In addition, write two essay questions; word the questions so that they can easily be turned into topic sentences.

Short-Answer Questions

1. _____

_____

2. _____

_____

3. _____

_____

4. _____

_____

5. _____

_____

Essay Questions

1. _____

_____

2. _____

_____

Follow-up: Write your questions on the board to discuss as a class.

Written follow-up: Prepare for the quiz by writing answers to the questions your class has proposed. You may have abbreviations in your notes, but do not use abbreviations other than standard ones like *U.S.* in your answers.

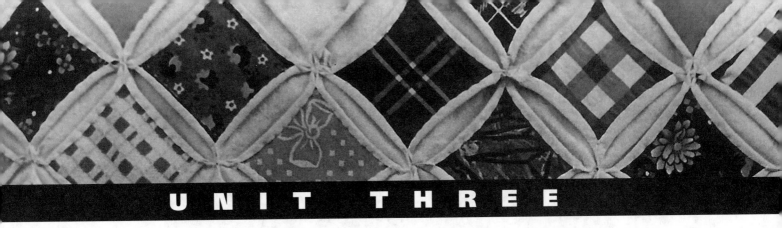

AMERICAN TRADEMARKS

Chapter 7. Multiculturalism

Chapter 8. Crime and Violence in the United States

Chapter 9. Technology: The Better Mousetrap

An industrial crucible

A patchwork quilt

MULTICULTURALISM 7

1. Prelistening Activities

A. Discussion

Discuss these questions with your classmates:

○ Why do you think the crucible and the patchwork quilt are often used as symbols of the multicultural character of United States society?

○ What does the crucible do to different metals mixed in it?

○ Is the quilt the same or a different symbol? How?

○ Is the culture of your country heterogeneous, as in the United States, or homogeneous?

B. Vocabulary and Key Concepts

Read through the sentences, trying to imagine which words would fit in the blanks. Then listen to a dictation of the full sentences, and write the missing words in the blanks.

1. I understand why a foreigner might react _____ to U.S. culture, especially if the person comes from a more ethnically

   and racially _____ society.

2. It seems naive or even perverse to _____ the

   existence of a culture that has such great _____
   on other cultures, for better or worse.

3. A _____ pot, literally a pot in which metals like aluminum and copper are melted in order to blend them, is the

   traditional _____ for the way the different groups of immigrants came together in the United States.

4. Some people feel that the monoculturalist view of many nationalities blending together into an _____ of all the parts in it is a _____.

5. Opponents point out that many groups have at times been _____ from participating in U.S. society through segregation and _____.

6. U.S. society probably did not assimilate new cultural input until the new immigrants were _____ with less _____.

7. The metaphor the multiculturalists use is the patchwork _____, a _____ of separate, autonomous subcultures.

8. A group that has traditionally _____ marrying outside its group, Jews, now has an _____ rate of 50%.

9. The point here is that the ethnically and racially pure individuals _____ by the multiculturalist view are more the _____ than the rule.

10. We _____ some of our culture from our families and _____ some of our culture unconsciously.

11. If _____ does not take place in the first _____, it most certainly does by the second or third.

12. Monoculturalists fear a _____, or even destruction, of U.S. culture, while _____ of the pluralistic view disagree.

13. It would be wrong to assume that the _____ culture we've been speaking about _____ the culture of only one group.

Follow-up: Check the spelling of the dictated words with your teacher. Discuss the meanings of these words and any other unfamiliar words in the sentences.

C. Predictions

Using the photographs and the vocabulary exercise as a starting point, write three questions that you think will be answered in the lecture.

Examples: ○ Is U.S. culture becoming more like the cultures of new immigrants?
○ Is American culture basically European?

1. _____

_____

2. _____

_____

3. _____

_____

Follow-up: After you have written your questions, share them with your teacher and your classmates.

D. Notetaking Preparation

1. Key Words: Listening

Work with a partner to practice taking down key words: nouns, verbs, adjectives, and adverbs. One partner will read *Vocabulary and Key Concepts* sentences 1–4 while the other takes notes. Then switch parts for sentences 5–8.

Follow-up: With your partner, test your key words by recalling all the information in the sentences from what you wrote. Your partner will check to see if you can recall the *message*, not necessarily the exact words. Then change roles and test your partner's key words.

2. Rhetorical Cues: Transition Words

Formal speech, like formal writing, is characterized by more frequent use of transition words and phrases. Transition words like *however, therefore,* and *in fact* help the listener understand the relationship between the lecturer's ideas. A good understanding of transition words will make a formal lecture more coherent to you. Test your knowledge of the italicized words on the next page by using them to complete the sentences in the exercise.

○ *Nevertheless, on the other hand,* and *however* all point out contrasts between two ideas.

○ *For instance* presents examples.

○ *In fact* is used for emphasis.

○ *Rather* is used like *instead.*

○ *Furthermore* is used like *also.*

a. The United States is not a racially homogeneous society;

_____, Japan is.

b. The melting pot metaphor is a very old one.

_____, it's been used for well over a century.

c. Culture comes to people in different ways.

_____, we inherit some, we absorb some, and we choose some.

d. There are many proponents of the multiculturalist view;

_____, I don't really agree with this view.

e. The multiculturalists don't use the metaphor of the melting pot.

_____, they use the patchwork quilt.

f. Monoculturalists fear a fragmentation of U.S. culture because of a massive Hispanic immigration. _____, pluralists see the bright side of this immigration.

g. There are two problems with this theory. Some existing groups were excluded from participating fully in society; _____, newly arrived groups were discriminated against.

Follow-up: Discuss your answers as a class.

2. Listening

A. First Listening

Listen for general ideas. The lecturer begins with some objections to current views of U.S. culture, views that she finds naive. The main part of the lecture is a discussion of three different views of multiculturalism, and these views might sound similar at first. However, they are quite different, if only in subtle ways. Listen for these three different views, and write them down under ST1, ST2, and ST3. Take down details you have time for, but make sure you take down the subtopics.

NOTES

Introduction:

ST1_____

ST2_____

ST3_____

Follow-up: Now check your major subtopics with your teacher.

B. Further Listening

While listening again, write down necessary relevant details below the main subtopic to which they belong. Remember to use key words to save time.

Follow-up: Check your notes. If you missed important information or have doubts about your notes, 1) verify them by asking a classmate questions to fill the gaps in your notes or 2) listen to the lecture a third time. When verifying your notes with a classmate, do not show each other your notes; ask specific questions to get the information you need.

Examples: ○   By any chance, did you catch what was said about the impact of U.S. culture on the world?
○   Could you help me out? What does "in all fairness" mean?

This is also a good time to check to see if the lecturer answered your *Predictions* questions about the lecture.

3. Postlistening Activities

A. Accuracy Check

Listen to the following questions, and write *short answers*. One question can be answered simply with *yes* or *no*. Use your notes. You will hear each question one time only.

1. _____

2. _____

3. _____

4. _____

5. _____

6. _____

7. _____

8. _____

9. _____

10. _____

Follow-up: Check your answers with your teacher. If your score is less than 70%, you may need to listen to the lecture again or rewrite your notes so that you can understand and retrieve the information in them.

B. Oral Activities

1. Review

In groups of four, use your notes to reproduce sections of the lecture. Student A will present the introduction, Student B subtopic 1, and so on. Check what you hear against your notes. If you don't understand or you disagree with what you hear, wait until your classmate finishes. Then bring your notes into agreement by seeking clarification, as follows:

○ I beg your pardon, but I didn't catch what you said about the impact of the United States on other countries.

○ I'm sorry. I don't believe I followed what you said about discrimination against certain groups.

2. Transfer

If your class is multinational, prepare a short oral report about the culture of your country, covering the points below. Work with the other students from your country.

If your classmates are all from your country, discuss the culture of your country as a class. Discuss these points:

○ Is your culture racially and ethnically homogeneous or heterogeneous?

○ How open is your culture to influences from other cultures? Do people who spend long periods of time in your country assimilate to the culture, or do they maintain their own cultures?

○ What metaphor do you think fits your culture?

C. Collaboration: Summary

In groups of three, with one member acting as secretary, write a one-paragraph summary of the lecture on multiculturalism. Use the guidelines below to decide which information to include. Write the answers in complete sentences in paragraph form, but limit your summary to 100 words.

1. Write a first general sentence that tells how many views of culture the lecturer mentions and tells whether the views are similar or different.

2. Characterize each view briefly. Mention the metaphor used to describe it as well as its main characteristics.

Follow-up: Exchange summaries with at least one other group. Find something you like in other groups' summaries. Alternatively, each group can read its summary to the class, which can then vote on the best one.

D. Pursuing the Topic

The following are recommended for a closer look at the multicultural nature of the United States:

Books/Periodicals

Postrel, Virginia I. "Uncommon Culture." *Reason*, May 1993, pp. 67–69.

Postrel discusses how and why assimilation takes place in the United States.

Rodriguez, Richard. *Days of Obligation: An Argument with My Mexican Father.* New York: Viking, 1992.

Rodriguez, born of Mexican immigrant parents, discusses his controversial views of U.S. multiculturalism.

Films/Videos

The Joy Luck Club, Wayne Wang, director; 138 minutes, R.

The movie charts the lives and loves of four Chinese immigrants and their American-born daughters.

Mississippi Masala, Mira Nair, director; 118 minutes, R.

The movie explores the lives of Asian Indians living in the rural U.S. South and their dealings with African American and white communities around them.

Interview

Interview a U.S. citizen to find out his or her views on multiculturalism. Beforehand, prepare questions as a class to ask

- O what the person's ethnic/racial background is
- O how the person feels that this background has influenced him or her
- O which metaphor makes the most sense to him or her
- O any other questions your class is interested in

Write down the answers to the questions, and share the information with your classmates.

Variation: Invite an American to visit your class, and have the whole class interview him or her, using the questions that you wrote.

CRIME AND VIOLENCE IN THE UNITED STATES

8

1. Prelistening Activities

A. Discussion

Discuss these questions with your classmates:

○ Who put up these signs, the police or private citizens?

○ What is the purpose of these signs?

○ Would you say there is more crime in the United States or in your country? Why?

B. Vocabulary and Key Concepts

Read through the sentences, trying to imagine which words would fit in the blanks. Then listen to a dictation of the full sentences, and write the missing words in the blanks.

1. For every _____ about crime, there seems to

   be a counter-theory that _____ it.

2. People are afraid of becoming _____ of violent

   crimes like robbery, _____, murder, and rape.

3. Statistics are harder to come by for _____-

   _____ crime, crimes including

   _____ and bribery.

4. One theory says that people are basically _____

    by nature and, therefore, _____

    _____ violence.

5. If a person commits a crime, society is _____

    _____ because society's

    _____ are the cause of the criminal behavior.

6. There are _____ causes like racism and more
    obvious causes like the breakdown of the family and a

    _____ of drugs.

7. Because they have been _____

    _____ the benefits that most Americans have,
    criminals are alienated from society, which causes them to

    _____ _____ at the
    society.

8. The _____ is that small part of the population
    which typically fits the following profile: poor, unemployed, badly

    educated, _____ black, inner-city youth, some
    of whom belong to gangs.

9. According to the theory, society _____ this

    aggressiveness and potential violence by _____ us.

10. Society gives us _____ against killing and
    stealing, for example, and values for honesty and

    _____.

11. If we are adequately socialized, we have a

    _____, the result of values that determine

    how we _____ _____
    our children.

12. The amount of crime depends on how _____

    is used as a _____ to crime—that is, how
    effectively the criminal justice system functions.

13. Typically, white-collar criminals, who include some businessmen and

_____, may be _____

a well-developed conscience.

14. Without a strong conscience, a person's innate aggressiveness

_____ _____ and

_____ _____ crime.

15. Many experts feel that this can come about only if the underclass has

the same _____ that the majority of the popu-

lation _____ _____

_____.

Follow-up: Check the spelling of the dictated words with your teacher. Discuss the meanings of those words and any other unfamiliar words in the sentences.

C. Predictions

Using the photographs and the vocabulary exercise as a starting point, write three questions that you think will be answered in the lecture.

Example: ○ How did the underclass in the United States develop?

1. _____

_____

2. _____

_____

3. _____

_____

Follow-up: After you have written your questions, share them with your teacher and your classmates.

D. Notetaking Preparation

1. Structuring

It is easier to *get* information from your notes if you make an effort to organize the ideas on the page as you *take* notes. Organizing the ideas means putting the ideas down in a logical way. The first step in organizing your ideas is to distinguish between main ideas and secondary ideas. Organize your notes by writing main ideas all the way to the left of the page and by writing secondary ideas a little to the right. Details can be indented even further to the right. Look at how the introduction to this lesson has been structured:

Looking into crime = proverbial can of worms
- many problems emerge
- every theory has counter-theory

Violent crime has increased in recent decades
- robbery, assault, murder
    murder rate doubled/30 years
    violent crime up 23%
- public afraid of becoming victims

a. How many main ideas are there in the introduction? What are they?

b. How many secondary points support the first main idea?

c. How many secondary points support the second main idea? What details support one of those secondary points? Where are these details written?

2. Rhetorical Cues

Read these sentences, in which the lecturer uses rhetorical cues to make a transition from one topic to another. Decide in which order you will hear them. Number them from first (1) to sixth (6).

_____ **a.** To start off with, liberals—in politics, sociology, and other fields—typically embrace the first theory.

_____ **b.** Actually, I feel that both theories serve us in identifying solutions.

_____ **c.** Crime is such a difficult issue to discuss because it can be looked at in so many different ways. Today I'd like to take a philosophical, sociological look at society and crime by discussing two theories of crime.

_____ **d.** In another lecture, we'll look at the justice system and why criminals very often think they won't get caught or punished for their crimes, but we don't have any more time today.

_____ **e.** So we need to look a little further into the causes of crime; let's look at the second theory.

_____ **f.** The second theory, often embraced by conservatives, sees people as innately aggressive and predisposed to violence.

Follow-up: Discuss your answers as a class.

2. Listening

A. First Listening

You already have notes for the introduction. Review those notes so that you can follow how the notetaker structured the information. Then use the first listening to take down the three major subtopics. As you take down additional information, structure it by putting main ideas to the left and indenting for secondary ideas and indenting even farther for details.

NOTES

Introduction:

ST1 _____

ST2  _____

ST3 _____

Follow-up: Now check your major subtopics with your teacher.

B. Further Listening

While listening again, write down necessary relevant details below the main subtopic to which they belong. Remember to structure the information as you take it down.

Follow-up: Check your notes. If you missed important information or have doubts about your notes, 1) verify them by asking a classmate questions to fill the gaps in your notes or 2) listen to the lecture a third time. When verifying your notes with a classmate, do not show each other your notes; ask specific questions to get the information you need.

Examples: ○ Do you have any idea whether liberals embrace the first theory or the second one?

   ○ I'm wondering if you caught *how* society socializes people.

This is also a good time to check to see if the lecturer answered your *Predictions* questions about the lecture.

3. Postlistening Activities

A. Accuracy Check

Listen to the following questions, and write *short answers*. Use your notes. You will hear each question one time only.

1. _____

2. _____

3. _____

4. _____

5. _____

6. _____

7. _____

8. _____

9. _____

10. _____

Follow-up: Check your answers with your teacher. If your score is less than 70%, you may need to listen to the lecture again or rewrite your notes so that you can understand and retrieve the information in them.

B. Oral Activities

1. Review

In groups of four, use your notes to practice giving one section of the lecture to classmates. Take turns practicing different sections until everyone has had a chance to speak. For example, Student A will give the introduction, Student B will give subtopic 1, and so on. Check what you hear against your notes. If you don't understand or you disagree with what you hear, wait until the speaker finishes. Then bring your notes into agreement by clarifying points of disagreement, as follows:

○ Would you mind repeating what you said about why crime is a difficult issue to discuss?

○ Excuse me. Can you tell me once again why society is to blame, according to the first theory?

2. Transfer

If your class is multinational, prepare a short oral report about the population of your country, covering the points below. Work with the other students from your country.

If your classmates are all from your country, discuss the population of your country as a class. Discuss these points:

○ How much crime is there in your country?

○ Is the crime rate increasing or decreasing?

○ What are the causes of crime?

○ What solutions would you propose to reduce crime?

C. Collaboration: Writing Answers to Essay Questions

On the quiz at the end of this unit, there will be short-answer questions and essay questions. You will answer the short-answer questions with a few words or a sentence or two. You will answer the essay questions with a complete English paragraph.

With a partner, plan and write essay answers to the questions on crime. One will write the answer down, but both partners will collaborate in forming the answers.

If you need to brush up on answering essay questions, refer to the guidelines in Unit 1, Chapter 2, p. 18.

Essay Questions

1. Contrast the two theories about the *causes* of crime in the United States.

2. Discuss how society socializes us, according to the second theory of crime.

Follow-up: Share your answers with at least one other group. Or share your answers orally as a class, and discuss the strengths in each answer.

D. Pursuing the Topic

The following are recommended for a closer look at crime in the United States:

Books/Periodicals

Van den Haag, Ernest. "How to Cut Crime." *National Review*, May 30, 1994, pp. 30–35.

The writer discusses solutions to rather than causes of crime in the United States.

Films/Videos

Boyz 'N the Hood, John Singleton, director; 111 minutes, R.

The film shows young African American males who live in a world where physical and psychological violence are a constant threat.

Of Mice and Men, Gary Sinise, director; 110 minutes, PG-13.

From a John Steinbeck novel, the film depicts the difficulties of two itinerant workers, one of whom commits a murder.

The Fugitive, Andrew Davis, director; 127 minutes, PG-13.

A remake of an earlier movie and a TV series, this film shows a falsely accused man who escapes the police to prove himself innocent of his wife's murder.

TECHNOLOGY: THE BETTER MOUSETRAP

1. Prelistening Activities

A. Discussion

Discuss these questions with your classmates:

❍ What do the man on the bicycle and the people leaving the airplane have in common?

❍ Which of these means of transportation might be described as "low tech" and which as "high tech"?

❍ Do people in your country welcome new technology?

❍ Do you see a negative side to technology, or is everything that technology brings us good?

B. Vocabulary and Key Concepts

Read through the sentences, trying to imagine which words would fit in the blanks. Then listen to a dictation of the full sentences, and write the missing words in the blanks.

1. I think it would be fair to say that in the eyes of the world, one of the

   _____ of the United States is its technology:

   new _____ and advanced procedures for solving problems.

2. To my mind, it is because Americans have generally

   _____ technology _____ progress.

3. People's _____ in technology was no doubt

   _____ because technology provided practical
   inventions that for the most part saved labor, time, money, and even
   lives.

4. In the factory, there was the automobile _____

   _____ and in medicine the development of

   antibiotics and _____ against serious diseases.

5. I suspect this loss of faith, this _____ about

   technology, came about when the U.S. was _____
   with some big problems that technology was not able to solve.

6. All of these problems occurred in the same decade, and they

   _____ Americans'

   _____ in technology, I think.

7. Today, I think it's fair to say that although their faith is largely

   _____, Americans are

   _____ about technology.

8. I think people are _____ when they think
   technology can solve social problems like crime, poor educational

   _____, and poverty.

9. Here we are talking about serious environmental problems like the

   _____ effect, depletion of the ozone layer,

   acid rain, and _____ waste.

10. This medical technology makes possible _____
    engineering as well as new techniques of human

    _____, birth control, and life support.

11. Is it right for parents to choose their child's genetic make-up by

    _____ _____ for

    physical _____ like eye color and nose shape?

12. Is it right to _____ a pregnancy if the

    _____ genes show that the child will have a
    serious disease or a mental deficiency?

13. Today, for better or worse, I think all countries are in the same boat

_____ - _____ -

_____ technology because problems in one

country can _____ neighboring countries.

Follow-up: Check the spelling of the dictated words with your teacher. Discuss the meanings of these words and any other unfamiliar words in the sentences.

C. Predictions

Using the photographs and the vocabulary exercise as a starting point, write three questions that you think will be answered in the lecture.

Example: ○   Is the state of the environment getting better or worse?

1. _____

_____

2. _____

_____

3. _____

_____

Follow-up: After you have written your questions, share them with your teacher and your classmates.

D. Notetaking Preparation

1. Structuring

In Chapter 8, you worked on structuring your notes to make them easier to read. Practice organizing ideas while listening by writing main ideas to the left, secondary ideas a little to the right, and details farther to the right. Listen to this passage from the lecture two times, and take notes using key words. Use the lines on the following page to structure your notes.

_____

_____

_____

_____

_____

_____

_____

Follow-up: Dictate your notes to another student or to your teacher, who will write the notes on the board with proper structuring.

2. Rhetorical Cues

Carefully read these sentences, which signal a transition to a new topic. Then decide in which order you will probably hear them in today's lecture. Number them from first (1) to fifth (5).

_____ **a.** Well, you'll have a chance to discuss these questions later, so let me finish up this lecture quickly.

_____ **b.** First let's take a look at technology in the United States in the distant past.

_____ **c.** These days, I think it's fair to say that Americans' faith is somewhat restored, but they are ambivalent about technology.

_____ **d.** Well, at any rate, there came a time in the 1960s and 1970s—and I'm shifting gears here a little—when a lot of Americans lost their faith in technology.

_____ **e.** Let's look into this ambivalence, case by case, a little further.

Follow-up: Discuss your answers as a class.

2. Listening

A. First Listening

Listen for general ideas. The lecturer gives a lengthy introduction, speculating about technology in the United States and the world. Then he presents his purpose in lecturing and explains how he will organize the lecture. He discusses the first two subtopics relatively briefly and goes into more detail in the third subtopic. The lecturer also makes some concluding remarks. As you listen, decide what his three main subtopics are, and write them down under ST1, ST2, and ST3. Take down details you have time for, but make sure that you take down the subtopics.

NOTES

Introduction:

ST1 _____

ST2 _____

Conclusion:

Follow-up: Now check your major subtopics with your teacher.

B. Further Listening

While listening again, write down necessary relevant details below the main subtopic to which they belong. Use key words to save time, and structure the information to organize your notes.

Follow-up: Check your notes. If you missed important information or have doubts about your notes, 1) verify them by asking a classmate questions to fill the gaps in your notes or 2) listen to the lecture a third time. When verifying your notes with a classmate, do not show each other your notes; ask specific questions to get the information you need.

Examples:
- ○ Did you understand what Americans are naive about?
- ○ How do Americans feel about technology and ethical problems?
- ○ Did you catch the third question about ethical problems?

This is also a good time to check to see if the lecturer answered your *Predictions* questions about the lecture.

3. Postlistening Activities

A. Accuracy Check

Listen to the following questions, and write *short answers* where possible. Use your notes. You will hear each question one time only.

1. _____

2. _____

3. _____

4. _____

5. _____

6. _____

7. _____

8. _____

9. _____

10. _____

Follow-up: Check your answers with your teacher. If your score is less than 70%, you may need to listen to the lecture again or rewrite your notes so that you can understand and retrieve the information in them.

B. Oral Activities

1. Review

In groups of four, use your notes to reproduce sections of the lecture. Student A will present the introduction; student B, subtopic 1; student C, subtopic 2; and student D, subtopic 3. Check what you hear against your notes. If you don't understand or you disagree with what you hear, wait until your classmate finishes. Then bring your notes into agreement by seeking clarification, as follows:

○ I didn't quite understand how Americans feel about technology today. Could you clarify what you said?

○ Can you explain again why the lecturer said we are all in the same boat vis-à-vis technology?

2. Transfer

As a class, discuss the *pros* and *cons* (advantages and disadvantages) of technology. Divide the blackboard in two: one part for advantages and the other for disadvantages. Individual students should write their arguments for or against technology in the proper place on the board. Then vote on the three strongest arguments for technology and the three strongest arguments against technology. Has anyone changed his or her position?

C. Collaboration: Discussion

Discuss one or two of the following questions with a partner. Then share your views with another pair or the whole class.

1. Is it right to terminate a pregnancy if the fetus's genes show that the child will have a serious disease or a mental deficiency? If the fetus is not the gender the parents want?

2. How long should we keep alive a patient who would die without high-tech machines?

3. How will the development of computer-controlled machines affect the total number of jobs? Will robots cause workers to lose jobs?

4. Most forms of pollution, such as acid rain and air pollution, are the direct result of technology like industrial processes and automobiles. Do you have faith that further technology can solve these problems? Or do we need to limit technology to control pollution?

D. Pursuing the Topic

The following are recommended for a closer look at the U.S. population:

Books/Periodicals

Brown, Lester, et al. *State of the World 1995.* New York: Norton, 1995.

Brown discusses the current state of the environment worldwide and what needs to be done to protect it.

Toffler, Alvin. *The Third Wave.* New York: Morrow, 1980.

Toffler discusses the nature of the information age and the changes in life and technology it causes worldwide.

Films/Videos

Sneakers, Phil Alden Robinson, director; 121 minutes, PG-13.

Young computer hackers begin by stealing from the rich to give to the poor and progress to more daring exploits.

Soylent Green, Richard Fleischer, director; 97 minutes, PG.

Made in 1973, this futuristic film portrays a grim 2022, where people eat synthetic food and are confronted with a deteriorating environment.

UNIT QUIZ DIRECTIONS

Now that you have completed from one to three chapters in this unit, your teacher may want you to take a quiz on the chapter(s). Your teacher will tell you whether or not you can use your notes to answer the questions on the quiz. If you can use your notes, review them before taking the quiz so that you can anticipate the questions and know where to find the answers. If you cannot use your notes on the quiz, *study them carefully before you take the quiz*, concentrating on organizing the information into main ideas and details that support these main ideas.

Work in small groups to help each other anticipate the questions your teacher will ask. Before breaking up into groups, review your notes and highlight important, noteworthy points. After reviewing your notes, break up into groups. Discuss and write specific short-answer questions and more general essay questions. (For guidelines in writing questions, see the Unit Quiz Directions at the end of Unit 1.)

Write your group's questions on the following pages.

Unit Quiz Preparation

Assign one group member to write down the questions; all members will help plan and compose the questions. For the lecture on multiculturalism, write five short-answer questions that can be answered with a few words or sentences. In addition, write two essay questions; word the essay questions so that they can easily be turned into topic sentences.

Short-Answer Questions

1. _____

_____

2. _____

_____

3. _____

_____

4. _____

_____

5. _____

_____

Essay Questions

1. _____

_____

2. _____

_____

Follow-up: Write your questions on the board to discuss as a class.

Written follow-up: Prepare for the quiz by writing answers to the questions your class has proposed. You may have abbreviations in your notes, but do not use abbreviations other than standard ones like *U.S.* in your answers.

Unit Quiz Preparation

Assign one group member to write down the questions; all members will help plan and compose the questions. For the lecture on crime, write five short-answer questions that can be answered with a few words or a maximum of two sentences. In addition, write two essay questions; word the essay questions so that they can easily be turned into topic sentences.

Short-Answer Questions

1. _____

   _____

2. _____

   _____

3. _____

   _____

4. _____

   _____

5. _____

   _____

Essay Questions

1. _____

   _____

2. _____

   _____

Follow-up: Write your questions on the board to discuss as a class.

Written follow-up: Prepare for the quiz by writing answers to the questions your class has proposed. You may have abbreviations in your notes, but do not use abbreviations other than standard ones like *U.S.* in your answers.

Unit Quiz Preparation

Assign one group member to write down the questions; all members will help plan and compose the questions. For the lecture on technology, write five short-answer questions that can be answered with a few words or sentences. In addition, write two essay questions; word the questions so that they can easily be turned into topic sentences.

Short-Answer Questions

1. _____

   _____

2. _____

   _____

3. _____

   _____

4. _____

   _____

5. _____

   _____

Essay Questions

1. _____

   _____

2. _____

   _____

Follow-up: Write your questions on the board to discuss as a class.

Written follow-up: Prepare for the quiz by writing answers to the questions your class has proposed. You may have abbreviations in your notes, but do not use abbreviations other than standard ones like *U.S.* in your answers.

EDUCATION

Flexibly structured primary
grade classroom

PUBLIC EDUCATION: PHILOSOPHY AND FUNDING 10

1. Prelistening Activities

A. Discussion

Discuss the following questions with your classmates:

○ What different kinds of activities are the children engaged in in this classroom?

○ Where is the teacher?

○ Do you think this is an American public or private school?

○ Does this classroom scene look similar to one you might see in your country?

B. Vocabulary and Key Concepts

Read through the sentences, trying to imagine which words would fit in the blanks. Then listen to a dictation of the full sentences, and write the missing words in the blanks.

1. Education in the United States is _____ until a certain age or grade level.

2. A small percentage of students attend private schools, either religious or _____, but most attend public schools.

3. Public education in the United States has _____ that often surprise foreigners.

4. There is no _____ _____

   or _____ examinations set by the government.

5. The _____ government influences public education by providing _____ for special programs such as education for the _____ and _____ education.

6. Control of education in the United States is mainly _____ _____ .

7. The state department of education _____ basic curriculum requirements and the number of _____ a high school student must have to graduate.

8. High school students take both required courses and _____ .

9. Each state has many school districts run by school boards whose members are _____ by voters of the district.

10. One responsibility of the local school district is the _____ of teachers and administrators.

11. Most funds for each school district come from residents of the district in the form of _____ .

12. During the nineteenth century there was _____ support and acceptance of public education as the best way to provide equal educational opportunity for all children.

13. People who have wanted to send their children to private religious schools have long questioned why they should have to pay taxes for public schools and private _____ at the same time.

14. All schools, public and private, would then _____ for the tuition dollars of these children.

15. There seems to be a _____ in society that our public education system is in trouble, and some changes will be necessary if public education is going to continue to be a _____ system for educating our children.

Follow-up: Check the spelling of the dictated words with your teacher. Discuss the meanings of these words and any other unfamiliar words in the sentences.

C. Predictions

Using the photograph and the vocabulary exercise as a starting point, write three questions that you think will be answered in the lecture.

Example: ○ What are the other responsibilities of the local school districts?

1. _____

_____

2. _____

_____

3. _____

_____

Follow-up: After you have written your questions, share them with your teacher and your classmates.

D. Notetaking Preparation

1. Structuring: Outlining

A good notetaker structures his or her notes. As you develop this skill, add numbers and letters to show the organization of your notes. Part of this chapter's lecture is presented here for you to practice this skill before you listen to the complete lecture. Complete the outline below with information from Subtopic 1. *Some* information is included in this outline to help keep you on track. Fill in the rest as you listen. Take a minute now to look over the outline to see where you need to fill in information.

ST1 Three levels of control

    A.

        1. sts basic curr.

        2.

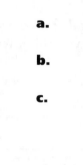

B. school district

    1. numbers depend on . . .

    2. responsibilities

        a.

        b.

        c.

C.

    1. teachers' responsibilities

        a.

        b.

2. Rhetorical Cues

Read the following sentences, which contain rhetorical cues to help you follow the organization of the lecture. Decide in which order you will hear them. Number them from first (1) to seventh (7).

_____ **a.** Local control of schools may seem very strange to some of you, but it will seem less strange if we consider how schools in the United States are funded.

_____ **b.** Control of education in the United States is mainly exercised locally at three levels. Let's begin with the state department of education.

_____ **c.** One interesting solution that has been suggested, among others, as an answer to the private school funding issue is the use of tuition vouchers.

_____ **d.** Finally, I'd like to discuss two issues related to the funding of schools that have been receiving a lot of attention recently in the States. The first deals with the inequality of educational opportunity that students face.

_____ **e.** The second level of control is the school district.

_____ **f.** The second issue is the issue of funding for private schools.

_____ **g.** The third level of control is the individual school itself.

2. Listening

A. First Listening

Listen for general ideas. After an introduction in which the lecturer mentions distinguishing features of public education in the United States, she goes on to discuss the three levels of control on education within each state. You already have notes on ST1 in Section 1 D.1. She then goes on to explain how funding contributes to local control. Finally, she discusses two important issues related to how public education is funded. As you listen, write the subtopics in the appropriate places and details you have time for. Structure your notes like the example in Section 1. D.1.

NOTES

Introduction:

ST1 _____

ST2 _____

ST3 _____

Follow-up: Check your major subtopics with your teacher before you listen to the lecture for the second time.

B. Further Listening

While structuring the notes, write down remaining relevant information.

Follow-up: Check your notes. If you missed important information or have doubts about your notes, 1) verify them by asking a classmate questions to fill the gaps in your notes or 2) listen to the lecture a third time. When verifying your notes with a classmate, do not show each other your notes; ask specific questions to get the information you need.

Examples: ○   Who is responsible for the hiring of teachers? Is it the school district or the individual school itself?
             ○   Where does the largest percentage of money for the public schools come from? Is it from the state or the local school district?

○   I didn't understand why some people think private schools are divisive. Do you have that in your notes?

This is also a good time to check to see if the lecturer answered your *Predictions* questions about the lecture.

3. Postlistening Activities

A. Accuracy Check

Listen to the following questions, and write *short answers*. You will hear each question one time only.

1. _____

2. _____

3. _____

4. _____

5. _____

6. _____

7. _____

8. _____

9. _____

10. _____

Follow-up: Check your answers with your teacher. If your score is less than 70%, you may need to listen to the lecture again or rewrite your notes so that you can understand and use them later.

B. Oral Activities

1. Review

In groups of four, use your notes to reproduce sections of the lecture. Student A will present the introduction, and Student B will present subtopic 1, including details. Student C will present subtopic 2 with details and Student D, subtopic 3 with details. Check what you hear against your notes. If you don't understand or you disagree with what you hear, wait until the speaker finishes. Then bring your notes into agreement by seeking clarification, as follows:

◯ Excuse me, can you tell me what two functions of the state government are?

◯ Could you repeat what you said about public education in the nineteenth century?

◯ I'm afraid my notes about taxes are different from yours.

2. Transfer

Discuss with a classmate how the educational system in your country is different from that in the United States. Try to use some of the ideas and vocabulary from Vocabulary and Key Concepts—for example, *nationwide curriculum, standardized examinations, required courses, electives, control, compulsory.*

C. Collaboration: Summary

Work with a partner, and use your notes to write a summary of the lecture in no more than 125 words. Be sure to include information about public and private schools, funding and control of schools, and current issues in U.S. public education.

Follow-up: Share your summary with at least one other pair. Tell the other pair what you particularly like about their summary.

D. Pursuing the Topic

The following are recommended for a closer look at public education issues in the United States:

Books/Periodicals

"A Voucher Plan for Crowded Schools." *The New York Times*, Oct. 24, 1993, Sec. 1, p. 34.

> *This news article reports that a middle-class suburban community is considering educational vouchers as a possible solution to cope with increased enrollment and budget constraints.*

Films/Videos

Stand and Deliver, Roman Menendez, director; 104 minutes, PG.

> *This film is based on the true story of a high school teacher who tried to inspire students and raise academic standards in a U.S. inner-city, minority neighborhood school.*

Dead Poets' Society, Peter Weir, director; 129 minutes, PG.

> *This film depicts the efforts of a teacher who uses poetry to inspire private preparatory school students to be more expressive and to "seize the moment," with unexpected dramatic results.*

Interview

Interview a U.S. citizen who attended public schools to find out his or her view on some of the issues highlighted in the lecture. Beforehand, write questions as a class to ask

○ the person's opinion of his or her public school education

○ what he or she thinks are the best and worst things about public schools

○ what the person thinks about tax money in the form of vouchers going to private schools

○ what he or she thinks about prayer in public schools

○ any other questions your class is interested in

Write down the answers to the questions, and share the information with your classmates.

Variation: Invite an American to visit your class, and have the whole class interview him or her using the questions that you wrote.

Field Trip

If you are studying in the States, it may be possible for your instructor to make arrangements for your class to visit a local public elementary, middle, or high school. Although the details of such visits have to be worked out with the school you visit, American students will be curious about your country and culture, so be prepared to answer questions.

POSTSECONDARY EDUCATION: ADMISSIONS* 11

1. Prelistening Activities

A. Discussion

Discuss the following questions with your classmates:

○ Do you think that this is an important examination that the students are taking?

○ What will happen if they fail this exam?

○ Do students in your country take a lot of exams? What are the most important exams they take?

B. Vocabulary and Key Concepts

Read through the sentences, trying to imagine which words would fit in the blanks. Then listen to a dictation of the full sentences, and write the missing words in the blanks.

1. _____ education in the United States includes

_____ as well as senior colleges, most of which

are _____.

2. To be _____, a college must meet certain

*For those of you living overseas who would like to or plan to attend an American college or university, we suggest that you write for a list of Overseas Educational Advising Centers available from the College Board, Office of International Education, 1717 Massachusetts Avenue NW, Washington DC 20036 , U.S.A.

_____ set by institutional and professional associations.

3. The more _____ private schools are more

_____—that is, they have stiffer admissions requirements.

4. All college applicants must submit a _____ of

high school grades and often _____ test results.

5. A student's _____ activities and possibly

_____ _____ are often factors in his or her admission.

6. Some freshmen _____

_____ of school after their first year rather

than _____ for a second year.

7. Some students begin college at a junior college with more

_____ admissions requirements and later

_____ to a senior college.

Follow-up: Check the spelling of the dictated words with your teacher. Discuss the meanings of these words and any other unfamiliar words in the sentences.

C. Predictions

Using the photograph and the vocabulary exercise as a starting point, write three questions that you think will be answered in the lecture.

Example: ○   How many colleges and universities are there in the U.S.?

1. _____

_____

2. _____

_____

3. _____

_____

Follow-up: After you have written your questions, share them with your teacher and your classmates.

D. Notetaking Preparation

1. Structuring: Listening

In the previous lesson we talked about *structuring* notes by using letters and numbers to make the notes clearer and easier to use. Practice structuring your notes as you listen to a portion of this lecture. Remember to move from left to right as you take down more specific information. The main idea, the most general one, is written for you.

ST3 Junior colleges differ from sen. colls.

   A.

    1.

   B.

    1.

    2.

   C.

    1.

    2.

Conclusion:

Follow-up: Compare your notes with another student's. Do you have the same information under A, B, and C?

2. Acronyms

Acronyms are abbreviations in which the first letters of the words in a phrase are used as a shortcut way to speak or write about the phrase. For example, ESL is an acronym for "English as a Second Language." It is often used in both spoken and written language.

In this lecture the following tests and degrees will be referred to in abbreviated form. As you now write the first-letter abbreviations, say them to yourself. When you take notes, use the abbreviations.

Tests and Degrees	Abbreviations
Graduate Record Examination	GRE
Graduate Management Admissions Test	
Law School Admissions Test	
Medical College Admissions Test	
Scholastic Aptitude Test	
Associate of Arts degree	A.A. degree
Bachelor of Science degree	
Bachelor of Arts degree	

2. Listening

A. First Listening

The lecturer appears to be in a hurry today to get into her topic. Her introduction is very brief and basically consists of an announcement of her three major subtopics. You will not need to take notes on the introduction itself. However, notice as you listen that the conclusion, which begins with "in brief," contains important logical conclusions about the three subtopics that you will want to include in your notes. As you take notes, take down details you have time for, but make sure that you take down the subtopics. Again, practice structuring your notes by using letters and numbers.

NOTES

ST1 _____

ST2 _____

ST3 _____

Conclusion:

Follow-up: Check your major subtopics with your teacher. Which subtopic would you look under to answer the following questions?

○ What are two factors that a college or university might use to decide whether to admit a student?

○ What is the range (from low to high) of the total cost of attending a college or university?

○ Where can you receive an Associate of Arts degree?

B. Further Listening

While continuing to structure your notes, write down remaining relevant information.

Follow-up: Check your notes. If you missed important information or have doubts about your notes, 1) verify them by asking a classmate questions to fill the gaps in your notes or 2) listen to the lecture a third time. When verifying your notes with a classmate, do not show each other your notes; ask specific questions to get the information you need.

Examples:
○ What does SAT stand for? Do all high school students have to take this exam before they can graduate?
○ What percentage of university students actually graduate?
○ What do you have in your notes about the differences between junior colleges and four-year colleges and universities? I'm not sure I got everything the lecturer said.

This is also a good time to check to see if the lecturer answered your *Predictions* questions about the lecture.

3. Postlistening Activities

A. Accuracy Check

Listen to the following questions, and write *short answers*. You will hear each question one time only.

1. _____

2. _____

3. _____

4. _____

5. _____

6. _____

7. _____

8. _____

9. _____

10. _____

Follow-up: Check your answers with your teacher. If your score is less than 70%, you may need to listen to the lecture again or rewrite your notes so that you can understand and use them later.

B. Oral Activities

1. Review

In small groups, review your notes section by section to be sure that all members have a complete set of notes for each subsection. At the end of this activity, your teacher will ask various class members to reproduce sections of the lecture for the whole class to listen to. At that time, check what you hear against your notes. If you don't understand or you disagree with what you hear, wait until the speaker finishes. Then bring your notes into agreement by seeking clarification, as follows:

○ Did you say that some schools have up to 15,000 or 50,000 students?

○ In my notes I have that it's expensive to attend a junior college. What do you have?

○ I'm not sure what it means to "drop out" of school.

2. Transfer

If you and your classmates come from different countries, discuss these questions with a partner or in small groups. If not, discuss them with the whole class.

○ How many colleges and universities are there in your country?

○ What kinds of colleges and universities do you have?

○ Where are these schools located—in major cities or in small towns?

○ Approximately how many students are there at these schools?

○ What percentage of high school graduates go on to a university?

Some countries take a more elitist approach to education than does the United States. That is, some countries limit the number of students who can go on to college by means of a highly competitive examination system. Discuss the following two questions in pairs, in small groups, or as a class:

○ What might be some of the social, political, and economic reasons for an elitist educational system?

○ What are the advantages and disadvantages of the two different approaches to education—elitist and non-elitist?

C. Collaboration: Writing Answers to Essay Questions

To help you prepare for the essay questions in the Unit Quiz at the end of this unit, plan and write essay answers to the following questions on U.S. postsecondary education in groups of three or four. Appoint one member of the group to do the actual writing; all members of the group should participate in planning and helping with the answers. At this point, you should refer to the guidelines in Unit 1, Chapter 2, p. 18. Review the guidelines before you begin to write essay answers.

Questions:

1. Discuss the wide variety of sizes, kinds, and locations of American universities and colleges.

2. Compare and contrast junior colleges and four-year universities.

Follow-up: Share your answers with at least one other group that has written on the same question(s). Or share your answers orally as a class, and discuss the strengths in each answer.

D. Pursuing the Topic

The following are recommended for a closer look at university admissions issues in the United States:

Books/Periodicals

Chance, Paul. "Testing Education: An Attack on the Scholastic Aptitude Test Unwittingly Reveals the Failure of American Schools." *Psychology Today*, May 1988, pp. 20-21.

> *Chance reviews* The Case Against the SAT *by James Crouse and Dale Trusheim, a book in which the authors claim the SAT is unnecessary. Chance's review discusses the arguments they make against the SAT.*

Interview

Interview an American high school senior who is planning to attend a college or university. Before the interview, prepare questions as a class to ask

○ how many schools the person is applying to and why he or she selected these particular schools

○ how important the person thinks the SAT score is (assuming he or she is taking the SAT)

○ how important the person thinks high school grades are in getting admitted

○ whether the person believes that extracurricular activities are important when a school considers an application for admission

○ any other questions your class is interested in

Write down the answers to the questions, and share the information with your classmates.

Variation: Invite an American to visit your class, and have the whole class interview him or her using the questions that you wrote.

UNIVERSITY LIFE 12

1. Prelistening Activities

A. Discussion

Discuss the following questions with your classmates:

○ Do you think these are typical classroom scenes you would see at an American university?

○ Which of these classes do you think is a graduate course?

○ Do these classrooms look like classrooms in your country?

○ How many hours a week do students have classes when they attend a university in your country?

B. Vocabulary and Key Concepts

Read through the sentences, trying to imagine which words would fit in the blanks. Then listen to a dictation of the full sentences, and write the missing words in the blanks.

1. The student body on a U.S. campus is diverse; one meets students of greatly different ages, from different racial and

   _____ _____, and from

   different _____ levels.

2. Let's begin by talking about an _____ student

   entering his or her _____ year.

3. Foreign students often find U.S. students less well-prepared for college than they expected. The U.S. students are often not very

   _____-_____ in inter-

   national matters or very _____-

   _____ about foreign countries.

4. To _____ how the average U.S. university class might be different, it will be helpful to begin by discussing the

_____ .

5. _____ dates of assignments, dates of exams,

and the teacher's _____

_____ are usually all found on the course syllabus.

6. A major difference in graduate school is that some classes are con-

ducted as _____, without exams and quizzes.

This is possible only with highly _____ and

_____ students, of course.

Follow-up: Check the spelling of the dictated words with your teacher. Discuss the meanings of these words and any other unfamiliar words in the sentences.

C. Predictions

Using the photographs and the vocabulary exercise as a starting point, write three questions that you think will be answered in the lecture.

Example: ○   How many classes do American university students have in one week?

1. _____

_____

2. _____

_____

3. _____

_____

Follow-up: After you have written your questions, share them with your teacher and your classmates.

D. Notetaking Preparation

1. Deciphering Notes

Sometimes you may for one reason or another miss a lecture and have to ask a classmate to share his or her notes. If your classmate has taken good notes, you may be able to reconstruct much of the message of a lecture.

Imagine that you missed a lecture in which your professor discussed some basic differences between U.S. colleges and universities and those in foreign countries. Because you were absent, you photocopied a class-mate's notes. See if you can use these notes to answer your teacher's questions. Work with a partner, if possible.

Educ. System in Coll. or Univ.

1. Kinds of courses

    a. required (sometimes choice among some req. courses = alternatives)

    b. elec. -- students choose

    c. prerequisites -- req. before another course can be taken

2. Schedule

    —very flexible

    —late afternoon/even. courses (working stud.)

3. Classes

    —diff. people class to class

    —great variety of kinds of peo. (difficult for some young freshmen from small homogeneous h. schools, big change)

Directions: Answer in complete sentences.

a. What are prerequisites?

b. What is the difference between an alternative class and an elective class?

c. Why are the same classes sometimes offered both during the day and in the late afternoon or evening?

d. Why do incoming freshmen from small high schools sometimes suffer from a kind of culture shock?

Follow-up: Check your answers with your teacher.

2. Rhetorical Cues

Read the following sentences, which contain rhetorical cues to help you follow the organization of the lecture. Decide in which order you will hear them. Number them from first (1) to sixth (6).

_____ **a.** Let's move on now to discuss student obligations in a typical American class.

_____ **b.** Now that you have some general idea of differences in the student body population, I'd like to talk a few minutes about what I think an average student is and then discuss what a typical class might be like.

_____ **c.** I hope that today's lecture has given you some idea about student life on an American campus and that you have noticed some differences between our system and yours.

_____ **d.** Let's begin by talking about an average student entering his or her freshman year.

_____ **e.** I have only a couple of minutes left, and I'd like to use them to talk about how graduate school is somewhat different from undergraduate school.

_____ **f.** Today I'd like to give you some ideas about how life at an American university or college might be different from the way it is in your country. To be sure, the student body on a U.S. campus is a pretty diverse group of people.

Culturegram: In this lecture you will hear the following words all used interchangeably to mean postsecondary education: _college, university, school._ The lecturer will use _high school_ when she is referring to secondary school. Otherwise, she is talking about postsecondary education.

2. Listening

A. First Listening

The lecturer begins with an introduction about the diversity of the student body at a typical American university or college. Listen for the signals that help you recognize when the lecturer is about to change to another major subtopic. Write down the main subtopics and as many of the relevant supporting details as possible. Continue to work on structuring your notes and using abbreviations and symbols.

NOTES

Introduction:

ST1

ST2 _____

ST3  _____

ST4 _____

Follow-up: Check your major subtopics with your teacher before you listen to the lecture for the second time.

B. Further Listening

Structure your notes as you take down remaining relevant information.

Follow-up: Check your notes. If you missed important information or have doubts about your notes, 1) verify them by asking a classmate questions to fill the gaps in your notes or 2) listen to the lecture a third time. When verifying your notes with a classmate, do not show each other your notes; ask specific questions to get the information you need.

Examples:
○ I didn't understand about undergraduate classes. Do most students have five hours of classes a day?
○ What did the lecturer say about quizzes?
○ Did the lecturer say that attendance in American university classes is optional?

This is also a good time to check to see if the lecturer answered your *Predictions* questions about the lecture.

3. Postlistening Activities

A. Accuracy Check

Listen to the following questions, and write *short answers*. You will hear each question one time only.

1. _____

2. _____

3. _____

4. _____

5. _____

6. _____

7. _____

8. _____

9. _____

10. _____

Follow-up: Check your answers with your teacher. If your score is less than 70%, you may need to listen to the lecture again or rewrite your notes so that you can understand and use them later.

B. Oral Activities

1. Review

In groups of five, use your notes to reproduce sections of the lecture. Student A will present the introduction. Student B will present Subtopic 1, including details. Student C will present Subtopic 2, and so on. Continue until all subsections, including their details, have been presented. Check what you hear against your notes. If you don't understand or you disagree with what you hear, wait until each group member has presented his or her section of the lecture. Then bring your notes into agreement by seeking clarification, as follows:

○ I don't think that the lecturer said there are exams in seminar classes.

○ Could you repeat what should be on a syllabus?

○ Do you understand the difference between graduate and undergraduate school?

2. Transfer

If you and your classmates come from different countries, discuss these questions with a partner or in small groups. If not, discuss them with the whole class.

- ○ How is your student body different from the student body in the United States?

- ○ What is an "average" student in your country like?

- ○ What is an "average" class like?

- ○ Approximately how many students are there at these schools?

- ○ How is the examination system different?

- ○ How do professors in your country conduct their classes?

- ○ How is graduate school different from undergraduate school?

C. Collaboration: Discussion

Discuss the following questions about general education issues in small groups. Appoint one person to report your group's opinions to the class.

1. Is it better for students to be evaluated by examinations or by some other way? What other ways could be used to evaluate students?

2. Should students evaluate their teachers? Why or why not?

3. Do students learn better from a strict, authoritarian teacher or from a friendly, democratic one? Why?

D. Pursuing the Topic

The following are recommended for a closer look at university admissions issues in the United States:

Books/Periodicals

Monaghan, Peter. "An All-Out Effort to Improve the Quality of Undergraduate Life." *The Chronicle of Higher Education*, Feb. 17, 1993, p. A25.

Falling enrollment and student dissatisfaction with college life led Regis University to implement several measures to help students socially, economically, and academically in order to boost student retention and graduation rates.

Levine, Daniel S. "Adult Students, Adult Needs." *The New York Times*, April 4, 1993, p.4A32

Levine discusses efforts colleges are making to meet both the practical and academic needs of older adults returning to college.

Interview

Interview an American university student. Before the interview, prepare questions as a class to ask

- general background information (age, hometown, major)

- whether he or she is a graduate or undergraduate student

- how many hours a week he or she is in class

- how large the classes are and whether they are lecture or discussion classes

- how much preparation his or her classes require

- whether he or she also has a job and, if so, how many hours a week he or she works

- any other questions your class is interested in

Write down the answers to the questions, and share the information with your classmates.

Variation 1: Invite an American to visit your class, and have the whole class interview him or her using the questions that you wrote.

Variation 2: If you are studying ESL at an American university, contact a professor from the department in which you plan to pursue your academic studies and ask if it is possible for you to attend one or two of his or her classes to get a better idea of how an American professor teaches.

UNIT QUIZ DIRECTIONS

Now that you have completed from one to three chapters in this unit, your teacher may want you to take a quiz on the chapter(s). Your teacher will tell you whether or not you can use your notes to answer the questions on the quiz. If you can use your notes, review them before taking the quiz so that you can anticipate the questions and know where to find the answers. If you cannot use your notes on the quiz, *study them carefully before you take the quiz*, concentrating on organizing the information into main ideas and details that support these main ideas.

Work in small groups to help each other anticipate the questions your teacher will ask. Before breaking up into groups, review your notes and highlight important, noteworthy points. After reviewing your notes, break up into groups. Discuss and write specific short-answer questions and more general essay questions. (For guidelines in writing questions, see the Unit Quiz Directions at the end of Unit 1.)

Write your group's questions on the following pages.

Unit Quiz Preparation

UNIT 4: CHAPTER 10

Assign one group member to write down the questions; all members will help plan and compose the questions. For the lecture on the philosophy and funding of public education, write five short-answer questions that can be answered with a few words or sentences. In addition, write two essay questions; word the questions so that they can easily be turned into topic sentences.

Short-Answer Questions

1. _____

_____

2. _____

_____

3. _____

_____

4. _____

_____

5. _____

_____

Essay Questions

1. _____

_____

2. _____

_____

Follow-up: Write your questions on the board to discuss as a class.

Written follow-up: Prepare for the quiz by writing answers to the questions your class has proposed. You may have abbreviations in your notes, but do not use abbreviations other than standard ones like *U.S.* in your answers.

Unit Quiz Preparation

Assign one group member to write down the questions; all members will help plan and compose the questions. For the lecture on postsecondary education, write five short-answer questions that can be answered with a few words or one or two sentences. In addition, write two essay questions; word the questions so that they can easily be turned into topic sentences.

Short-Answer Questions

1. _____

_____

2. _____

_____

3. _____

_____

4. _____

_____

5. _____

_____

Essay Questions

1. _____

_____

2. _____

_____

Follow-up: Write your questions on the board to discuss as a class.

Written follow-up: Prepare for the quiz by writing answers to the questions your class has proposed. You may have abbreviations in your notes, but do not use abbreviations other than standard ones like *U.S.* in your answers.

Unit Quiz Preparation

Assign one group member to write down the questions; all members will help plan and compose the questions. For the lecture on university life, write five short-answer questions that can be answered with a few words or one or two sentences. In addition, write two essay questions; word the questions so that they can easily be turned into topic sentences.

Short-Answer Questions

1. _____

_____

2. _____

_____

3. _____

_____

4. _____

_____

5. _____

_____

Essay Questions

1. _____

_____

2. _____

_____

Follow-up: Write your questions on the board to discuss as a class.

Written follow-up: Prepare for the quiz by writing answers to the questions your class has proposed. You may have abbreviations in your notes, but do not use abbreviations other than standard ones like *U.S.* in your answers.

THE OFFICIAL SIDE

Hoover Dam on the
Colorado River between
Arizona and Nevada

THE ROLE OF GOVERNMENT IN THE ECONOMY

13

1. Prelistening Activities

A. Discussion

Discuss the following questions with your classmates:

○ What purpose or purposes do dams serve?

○ Do you think this dam was built by a private company or by the U.S. government?

○ What kinds of things does your government build in your country?

○ Does your government play an active role in your economy?

B. Vocabulary and Key Concepts

Read through the sentences, trying to imagine which words would fit in the blanks. Then listen to a dictation of the full sentences, and write the missing words in the blanks.

1. One of the important characteristics of American-style capitalism is

   individual _____ of

   _____, including such things as houses and
   land, businesses, and intellectual property such as songs, poems,
   books, and inventions.

2. The second characteristic is _____

   _____.

3. The idea in a pure capitalistic system is for the government not to

_____, that is, for the government to take a

_____-_____ attitude.

4. In a pure capitalistic system, the government's role would be severely
limited. It would be responsible only for laws governing

_____ and property, as well as for the

_____ _____ .

5. Companies may have to install pollution _____

equipment to _____ _____
government regulations.

6. People who earn little or no _____ can receive

_____ _____, often

called _____ .

7. The government makes sure that the marketplace stays

_____ through its _____

and _____ laws.

8. The government interferes with the economy in an effort to maintain

_____ .

9. Through _____, the government tries to

control _____ .

10. The government has to be very careful to keep _____

and inflation in _____, however.

11. The government further tries to achieve stability through its

_____ and by controlling the

_____ rate.

Follow-up: Check the spelling of the dictated words with your teacher.
Discuss the meanings of these words and any other unfamiliar words in
the sentences.

C. Predictions

Using the photograph and the vocabulary exercise as a starting point, write three questions that you think will be answered in the lecture.

Example: ○   How does the government make sure that businesses obey environmental protection regulations?

1. _____

_____

2. _____

_____

3. _____

_____

Follow-up: After you have written your questions, share them with your teacher and your classmates.

D. Notetaking Preparation

1. Prelecture Reading

Most U.S. college and university teachers plan their lectures assuming that students will have read assigned chapters before class. To prepare for this chapter's lecture, read the following text describing the ongoing debate about the role of the government, and answer the questions that follow. Notice that a distrust of the government has been seen in all aspects of American politics and economic life since the days of the colonies; however, this text focuses on the debate about the role of the government in the economic life of the country.

Text:

Americans have been debating the role of the federal government ever since the American Revolution in the 1770s. The thirteen original colonies, which banded together to declare their independence from Britain, were very suspicious of a strong central government and protective of their individual rights as states. The Confederation government they formed saw the thirteen original colonies through the Revolution.

A few years after the end of the war, though, the Confederation was unable to solve many problems facing the new nation, and the need for a stronger central government led to a new Constitution, which expanded the power of the national government. Still, the debate about the role of government went on in many areas, including the economic sphere. Thomas Jefferson, third President, was a believer in laissez-faire economics; that is, he believed the government should not interfere in the economy. His general philosophy was "Government that governs least, governs best."

But by today's standards, the role of the national, or federal, government in the economy was very small, consisting largely of setting tariffs and excise taxes as well as issuing currency. It wasn't until the time of the Civil War in the 1860s that the first income tax was instituted. Before that time, the government did not have money for internal improvements to the country.

After that time, the government began to expand its role in the economy. The Industrial Revolution, which was occurring at the same time, led to demands for the government to expand its role in the regulation of railroads and other big business. During these years the government tended to take the side of big business rather than the side of organized labor. During the early years of the twentieth century, the government began to debate its role in the economy more sharply. President Theodore Roosevelt and President Woodrow Wilson took steps toward controlling the excessive power of big business.

However, it was the Great Depression of the 1930s that led most people to give up the idea of a laissez-faire economy. President Franklin Roosevelt led the government to take an increased role in the welfare of the people. His "New Deal" instituted programs by which the government provided employment for large numbers of unemployed people and provided welfare for others. His administration also instituted the Social Security system, by which workers pay into a fund that then provides a kind of insurance protection for older, retired workers and disabled workers. In the years following the New Deal, the role of the government in the economy continued to expand. During the 1960s there emerged a new conservative viewpoint, and efforts were made by many in politics to loosen the control of the government on the economy and to return to a more laissez-faire economy. This issue is still being debated.

Questions:

a. Did the thirteen original colonies want a strong central government? Explain.

b. Why was a new Constitution necessary a few years after the end of the Revolution?

c. What role does the government have in the economy in a laissez-faire economy?

d. How did the Civil War enable the government to expand its power over the economy?

e. Between the Civil War and the Great Depression, which side, big business or organized labor (workers), did the government usually take whenever there were conflicts?

f. What programs did the Roosevelt administration carry out in response to the Great Depression?

Follow-up: Discuss your answers with your teacher.

2. Rhetorical Cues

Read the following sentences, which contain rhetorical cues to help you follow the organization of the lecture. Decide in which order you will hear them. Number them from first (1) to seventh (7).

_____ **a.** In truth, because the United States is not a pure capitalistic system, government today does not maintain a completely laissez-faire attitude toward business.

_____ **b.** The first reason the government tries to regulate the economy is to protect the environment.

_____ **c.** Let me begin today by saying that the American economy is basically a capitalistic economy. One of the important characteristics of American-style capitalism is individual ownership of property.

_____ **d.** The last reason for the government's interfering with the economy is to maintain economic stability.

_____ **e.** The second characteristic is free enterprise.

_____ **f.** The second reason the government interferes with the economy is to help people who for some reason beyond their control earn little or no income.

_____ **g.** The third characteristic is free competitive markets.

Follow-up: Check your answers with your teacher.

2. Listening

A. First Listening

In the introduction the lecturer discusses how a *pure* capitalist government would function in order to point out how the United States is *not* a pure capitalist country, and then he goes on to explain *why* the government interferes. Notice that the lecturer starts out with the simpler reasons and finishes with the most complex. Take down as many relevant details as possible, but be sure to take down subtopics. Continue to work on structuring your notes and using abbreviations and symbols.

Introduction:

ST1 _____

ST2 _____

ST3 _____

ST4 _____

Follow-up: Check your major subtopics with your teacher before you listen to the lecture for the second time.

B. Further Listening

While listening again, write down necessary relevant details below the main subtopics to which they belong. Remember to structure your notes to make them easier to use later.

Follow-up: Check your notes. If you missed important information or have doubts about your notes, 1) verify them by asking a classmate questions to fill the gaps in your notes or 2) listen to the lecture a third time. When verifying your notes with a classmate, do not show each other your notes; ask specific questions to get the information you need.

Examples: ❍ How does the government try to help people who don't have enough money? I couldn't catch the names of the programs. Do you have them?
  ❍ Did you get why the government lowers the interest rate?

This is also a good time to check to see if the lecturer answered your *Predictions* questions about the lecture.

3. Postlistening Activities

A. Accuracy Check

Listen to the following questions, and write *short answers*. You will hear each question one time only.

1. _____
2. _____
3. _____
4. _____
5. _____
6. _____
7. _____
8. _____
9. _____
10. _____

Follow-up: Check your answers with your teacher. If your score is less than 70%, you may need to listen to the lecture again or rewrite your notes so that you can understand and use them later.

B. Oral Activities

1. Review

In small groups, review your notes, section by section, to be sure that all members have a complete set of notes for each subsection. At the end of this activity, your instructor will ask various class members to reproduce sections of the lecture for the whole class to listen to. At that time, check what you hear against your notes. If you don't understand or you disagree with what you hear, wait until the speaker finishes. Then bring your notes into agreement by seeking clarification, as follows:

○ Excuse me, I didn't catch what you said about free enterprise.

○ You said that raising taxes raises the inflation rate. I think it lowers it.

2. Transfer

If you and your classmates come from different countries, discuss these questions with a partner or in small groups. If not, discuss them with the whole class.

○ Is the government basically laissez-faire, or does it take an active role in the economy?

○ Does the government provide welfare, that is, help people who do not have enough money?

○ Does the government provide medical care, or must people pay for it?

○ Does the government regulate businesses in order to protect the environment?

C. Collaboration: Summary

In pairs, write a one-paragraph summary of the lecture. Include the main ideas from each of the main subtopics. Include important secondary points, but do not exceed 125 words.

Follow-up: Exchange summaries with at least one other pair. Find two things you like about the other summary.

D. Pursuing the Topic

The following are recommended for a closer look at the role of government in the United States:

Books/Periodicals

Clinton, Bill, and Gingrich, Newt. "What Good is Government . . . And Can We Make It Better?" *Newsweek*, April 10, 1995, pp. 26-28.

> *U.S. President Clinton and his political opponent Newt Gingrich express philosophically different ideas on the role and effectiveness of government in America today.*

Interview

Interview a U.S. citizen to find out his or her views on some of the issues highlighted in the lecture. Beforehand, write questions as a class to ask

○ what the person thinks is the primary responsibility of government

○ what the person thinks about tax money in the form of welfare going to unemployed healthy adults

○ whether he or she thinks the government is doing enough to protect the environment

○ any other questions your class is interested in

Write down the answers to the questions, and share the information with your classmates.

Variation: Invite an American to visit your class, and have the whole class interview him or her using the questions that you wrote.

Washington Star-News

Yield Tapes, Nixon Ordered
In 8 to 0 High Court Decision

"...To ensure that justice is done"

Hogan May Quit Md. Race
Under fire on Nixon issue

Trend Quickens
to Impeachment

Impeachment Issue C...

Athens Celebr...
New Civilian R...

GOVERNMENT BY CONSTITUTION: SEPARATION OF POWERS/CHECKS AND BALANCES

14

1. Prelistening Activities

A. Discussion

Discuss the following questions with your classmates:

○ Do you remember the name of the political scandal the newspaper headline is related to?

○ Find the word "impeachment" in the photograph. What do you think this word means?

○ What city do you think this is?

○ What kind of building is this man standing in front of?

○ Who makes the laws in your country?

○ If people in your country feel a law is unfair or unjust, what do they do?

B. Vocabulary and Key Concepts

Read through the sentences, trying to imagine which words would fit in the blanks. Then listen to a dictation of the full sentences, and write the missing words in the blanks.

1. Two important principles of the United States Constitution are the

_____ of powers and the system of

_____ and _____.

2. The Constitution provides for three _____ of

government: the _____, the executive, and the

_____ .

3. The legislative branch is primarily responsible for

_____ , or making, new laws. The executive
branch executes laws by signing them and by seeing that they are

_____ .

4. The judicial branch deals with those who are

_____   _____

_____ a law or who are involved in a

_____   _____ .

5. The judicial branch also handles _____ and
reviews existing laws to make sure they are

_____   _____ the U.S.
Constitution.

6. Each branch has its specific _____ and its own

particular power, which it must not _____ .

7. The presidential _____

_____   _____ is an
obvious example of checks and balances.

8. Because it's difficult for Congress to _____ a

presidential veto, the veto may _____

_____   _____

_____ this new law forever.

9. Although President Nixon was _____ of
illegal activities, he was never removed from office by Congress

because he _____ .

10. By finding laws against abortion _____ , the

Supreme Court in effect made abortion _____ .

11. In the area of _____ _____,
the Supreme Court declared it illegal to practice

_____ _____ in any form.

12. Probably the most important effect of this change was the

_____ of public schools.

13. After the President _____

_____ _____ for the

Supreme Court, the Congress must _____ his
choice.

Follow-up: Check the spelling of the dictated words with your teacher.
Discuss the meanings of these words and any other unfamiliar words in
the sentences.

C. Predictions

Using the photograph and the vocabulary exercise as a starting point,
write three questions that you think will be answered in the lecture.

Example: ○   Which branch of government is the president part of?

1. _____

_____

2. _____

_____

3. _____

_____

Follow-up: After you have written your questions, share them with
your teacher and your classmates.

D. Notetaking Preparation

1. Prelecture Reading

As we have mentioned in previous lessons, U.S. university students most
often prepare for each class by reading a text chapter, an article, or even a
case study. This preparation makes the instructor's lecture, usually on a
topic related to the reading, easier to follow and to take notes on.

Before listening to the lecture, read the following passage carefully and
answer the comprehension questions. You will notice how this preparation
will aid your comprehension of the lecture.

Judicial Review

Judicial review is the power of a court to invalidate or overturn any law passed by the legislature that the court believes to be unconstitutional. The concept of judicial review as exercised by the Supreme Court of the United States is almost unique in the world. It can be called an American invention. Nowhere else does the judiciary of a country exercise final say over laws passed by the legislature. This enormous power of judicial review by the Supreme Court was established in a famous case several years after the Constitution was written, *Marbury v. Madison* (1803). The Court's opinion stated that the Constitution was superior to any acts by the legislature and that it was the Court's duty to void any laws that went against the Constitution. This power was not explicitly expressed in the Constitution, and even today, almost 200 years later, the Supreme Court's power to void laws passed by the legislature is still controversial.

If we compare judicial review in the United States with that in a few other countries, we will see just how unusual it is. In Great Britain, the right of Parliament (the legislature) to make any law it wants to cannot be challenged by the courts. The courts can *interpret* but not determine the validity of a law. In Germany, the judiciary actually has had such power since shortly after World War II, but it has been slow to exercise judicial review for cultural and historical reasons. The judiciary in Canada has had this power since 1982, but whether it will exercise it in a way similar to that exercised by the U.S. Supreme Court cannot be known yet.

Questions:

a. What is judicial review?

b. Is judicial review guaranteed by the United States Constitution? Explain.

c. Which of the following countries has no provisions for judicial review—Britain, Canada, or Germany?

d. Do Germany and Canada exercise judicial review more or less frequently than the United States does? Explain.

Follow-up: Check your answers with your teacher before you continue.

2. Practicing the Language of Political Science

The following exercise will help you learn language used when discussing the separate powers that each branch of the U.S. government has and the *checks and balances* that each branch has over the other two branches. Look over the schematic, which shows *some* of the powers that each branch has and how some of these powers specifically limit the powers of the other two branches. Then answer the questions that follow the schematic.

The U.S. Government

Executive Branch	**Legislative Branch**	**Judicial Branch**
○ Sends suggestions to Congress (i.e., proposes new legislation)	○ Approves federal budget	○ Interprets laws
○ May veto bills sent by Congress for signature	○ Approves treaties	○ May declare a law unconstitutional
○ Nominates judges	○ Sends bills it has passed to President for signature	○ Interprets treaties
○ Makes treaties with other countries	○ May override veto by 2/3 majority	
○ Prepares federal budget	○ Must approve appointment of judges	
	○ May impeach the President	
	○ May impeach judges	

Work with a partner to answer these questions:

a. Which powers in each branch are checked by another branch?

b. Which powers seem to have no checks against them?

Follow-up: Check your answers with your classmates.

2. Listening

A. First Listening

The lecturer begins with a brief discussion of the Constitution of the United States and tells you its two guiding principles. She then announces her first subtopic, the three branches of the U.S. government. She goes on to explain the two guiding principles. Finally, she expands on the second principle with several examples and illustrations. (You will need to use the notetaking skills that you have learned so far to organize your notes on the blank notetaking page.)

Follow-up: Check your subtopics with your teacher. How did you organize your notes? Yours may be different from another student's. What is important is that your notes reflect the basic organization and information of the lecture.

B. Further Listening

While listening again, write down necessary relevant details below the main subtopics to which they belong.

Follow-up: Check your notes. If you missed important information or have doubts about your notes, 1) verify them by asking a classmate questions to fill the gaps in your notes or 2) listen to the lecture a third time. When verifying your notes with a classmate, do not show each other your notes; ask specific questions to get the information you need.

Examples: ○ What does the judicial system do? Do you have that in your notes?
○ I don't have anything in my notes about who chooses the people on the Supreme Court. Do you have it in your notes?
○ What can the President do if he doesn't like a law that the Congress sends him to sign? I didn't catch that word.

This is also a good time to check to see if the lecturer answered your *Predictions* questions about the lecture.

3. Postlistening Activities

A. Accuracy Check

Listen to the following questions, and write *short answers*. You will hear each question one time only.

1. _____

2. _____

3. _____

4. _____

5. _____

6. _____

7. _____

8. _____

9. _____

10. _____

Follow-up: Check your answers with your teacher. If your score is less than 70%, you may need to listen to the lecture again or rewrite your notes so that you can understand and use them later.

B. Oral Activities

1. Review

In small groups, discuss your notes, section by section, to be sure that all members have a complete set of notes for each subsection. At the end of this activity, your instructor will ask various class members to reproduce sections of the lecture for the whole class to listen to. At that time, check what you hear against your notes. If you don't understand or you disagree with what you hear, wait until the speaker finishes. Then bring your notes into agreement by seeking clarification, as follows:

❍ Did you say that Congress can veto a law? My notes say that the President can veto a law.

❍ Excuse me, could you repeat what you said about Watergate?

2. Transfer

If you and your classmates come from different countries, discuss these questions with a partner or in small groups. If not, discuss them with the whole class.

a. How is the power to make and enforce laws in your country divided? Explain.

b. Can a law be overturned by the judicial branch in your country? If so, under what circumstances?

c. Do you think the legislative branch of a government should have the power to remove the president of a country from office?

C. Collaboration: Writing Answers to Essay Questions

To help you prepare for the essay questions in the Unit Quiz at the end of this unit, plan and write essay answers to the following questions on the Constitution and the separation of powers. Work in groups of three or four. Appoint one member of the group to do the actual writing; all members of the group should participate in planning and helping with the answers.

Questions:

1. List the three branches of the U.S. government and describe their primary duties.

2. What are the two guiding principles of the U.S. Constitution, and what is their purpose?

Follow-up: Share your answers with at least one other group that has written on the same question(s). Or share your answers orally with the class, and discuss the strengths in each answer.

D. Pursuing the Topic

The following are recommended for a closer look at issues related to the Constitution of the United States:

Books/Periodicals

TIME, July 6, 1987.

> *This issue commemorates the 200th anniversary of the American Constitution. Numerous articles and essays discuss various aspects of and issues involved with the Constitution, among them its history and impact, landmark Supreme Court decisions, and current issues.*

Films/Videos

All the President's Men, Alan J. Pakula, director; 138 minutes, PG.

> *This film is based on the true story of two investigative reporters who broke the story of the Watergate scandal, which eventually brought down the Nixon administration.*

Interview

Interview a U.S. citizen who attended public schools to find out his or her views on some of the issues highlighted in the lecture. Beforehand, write questions as a class to ask

- O the person's opinion of his or her public school education

- O what he or she thinks are the best and worst things about public schools

- O what the person thinks about tax money in the form of vouchers going to private schools

- O what he or she thinks about prayer in public schools

- O any other questions your class is interested in

Write down the answers to the questions, and share the information with your classmates.

Variation: Invite an American to visit your class, and have the whole class interview him or her using the questions that you wrote.

COMMON LAW AND THE JURY SYSTEM

15

1. Prelistening Activities

A. Discussion

Discuss the following questions with your classmates:

○ Have you seen scenes of American courtrooms in movies or on TV?

○ Do you think they realistically depict what happens in courtrooms?

○ How are courtrooms different in your country?

B. Vocabulary and Key Concepts

Read through the sentences, trying to imagine which words would fit in the blanks. Then listen to a dictation of the full sentences, and write the missing words in the blanks.

1. The average person in the legal profession would probably say it's better to let a dozen _____ people go free than to punish one innocent person _____.

2. The guiding principle for the U.S. legal system is that an accused person is _____ _____ _____ _____ _____.

3. Under civil law the judge consults a complex _____ _____ _____ to decide whether the defendant is guilty and, if so, what sentence to give.

4. Under _____ _____

the judge considers the _____ set by other
court decisions.

5. The jury's responsibility is to hear _____ in

either civil or criminal trials and reach a _____ .

6. The judge guides the jurors by deciding what evidence is allowed and

by _____ _____

_____ by lawyers and witnesses.

7. In a criminal trial, if jurors are not convinced that the defendant is

guilty _____ _____

_____ , they must _____

him or her.

8. If the required number of jurors doesn't agree on a verdict, it is a

_____ _____ , and the

law requires a new _____ .

9. What happens in plea bargaining is that the accused

_____ _____ to a

_____ _____ .

Follow-up: Check the spelling of the dictated words with your teacher.
Discuss the meanings of these words and any other unfamiliar words in
the sentences.

C. Predictions

Using the photograph and the vocabulary exercise as a starting point,
write three questions that you think will be answered in the lecture.

Example: ○ How many people are on a jury?

1. _____

_____

2. _____

_____

3. _____

_____

Follow-up: After you have written your questions, share them with your teacher and your classmates.

D. Notetaking Preparation

1. Prelecture Reading

Before listening to a rather difficult lecture on the U.S. legal system, read a related passage dealing with *precedents* and surrogate motherhood, and then answer the comprehension questions that follow. Although somewhat difficult, the reading and the questions will prepare you for the lecture you will hear later.

The Baby M Case

The Baby M case became a controversial legal case in the United States in 1988. At issue were Baby M's custody and the validity of a contract. The contract provided that a woman, the surrogate mother, would have a baby for an infertile couple by artificial insemination of the husband's sperm and would receive payment for this service. Certainly, Baby M was not the first baby born to a surrogate mother, but in this case the surrogate mother, Mary Beth Whitehead-Gould, changed her mind after the baby was born and did not want to give the baby up, as she had agreed to do in the contract. The Sterns, the couple who had contracted for the baby, insisted that Ms. Whitehead-Gould fulfill the terms of the contract, and they took her to court. The New Jersey Supreme Court ruled that this type of contract was against public policy (the good of the general public) and, therefore, could not be enforced. (However, the court did award *custody* of the baby to the biological father. The mother, Ms. Whitehead-Gould, was awarded limited visitation rights.) This particular ruling was very important because there had been no previous court decision of this type at the level of a state supreme court. Therefore, this decision establishes a precedent for other states when they have to deal with the issue of surrogacy.

Questions:

a. Are Baby M's natural mother and father married to each other?

b. Who wanted to break the contract, Mary Beth Whitehead-Gould or the Sterns?

c. In this reading, *precedent* most nearly means

    1. a reason not to do something

    2. a decision used as a standard

    3. proof of innocence

    4. proof of guilt

d. Was there a precedent for judging surrogacy contracts before the Baby M case?

e. In what sense will the Baby M case serve as a precedent in the future?

Follow-up: Discuss your answers with your teacher before you continue.

2. Courtroom Language

Look at the following illustration of a typical courtroom scene. Work with a partner to answer the following questions.

a. Who keeps a written record of what is said in court?

b. Who ensures that the trial is conducted according to the law?

c. Who is a person who has knowledge of the case and is called to testify in court?

d. Who deliberates on the facts of the case and delivers a verdict (decision)?

e. Who has custody of prisoners and maintains order in the court?

f. Who is the person against whom the court action has been taken?

g. Who initiates court action against the defendant?

h. Who takes care of records involved in the court case?

Follow-up: Check your answers with your teacher.

2. Listening

A. First Listening

The lecturer begins with a rather long introduction in which she attempts to provide some background to a rather technical discussion of the U.S. legal system, which is based on common law. She then goes on to discuss the jury system and, finally, plea bargaining. It is not necessary to take notes until she begins to compare common law to civil law. Use the note-taking skills that you have practiced to make a set of meaningful and usable notes.

NOTES

Follow-up: Check your subtopics with your teacher. How did you organize your notes? Yours may be different from another student's. What is important is that your notes should reflect the basic organization and information of the lecture.

B. Further Listening

While listening again, write down necessary relevant details below the main subtopics to which they belong.

Follow-up: Check your notes. If you missed important information or have doubts about your notes, 1) verify them by asking a classmate questions to fill the gaps in your notes or 2) listen to the lecture a third time. When verifying your notes with a classmate, do not show each other your notes; ask specific questions to get the information you need.

Examples:
- What is the difference between common law and civil law? Do you have that in your notes?
- I don't have anything in my notes about what a judge does. Do you have it in your notes?

This is also a good time to check to see if the lecturer answered your *Predictions* questions about the lecture.

3. Postlistening Activities

A. Accuracy Check

Listen to the following questions, and write *short answers*. You will hear each question one time only.

1. _____
2. _____
3. _____
4. _____
5. _____
6. _____
7. _____
8. _____
9. _____
10. _____

Follow-up: Check your answers with your teacher. If your score is less than 70%, you may need to listen to the lecture again or rewrite your notes so that you can understand and use them later.

B. Oral Activities

1. Review

In small groups, discuss your notes, section by section, to be sure that all members have a complete set of notes for each subsection. At the end of this activity, your instructor will ask various class members to reproduce sections of the lecture for the whole class to listen to. At that time, check what you hear against your notes. If you don't understand or you disagree with what you hear, wait until the speaker finishes. Then bring your notes into agreement by seeking clarification, as follows:

○ Would you please repeat what you said about a written code of laws?

○ Excuse me, but you didn't mention plea bargaining. I think it's important.

2. Transfer

If your class is multinational, prepare a short oral report about the legal system of your country, comparing and contrasting it to the legal system of the United States. Work with other students from your country.

If your classmates are all from your country, discuss the similarities and differences as a class.

C. Collaboration: Discussion

Discuss these questions in small groups. Appoint one person to report your group's responses for each question to the class.

1. Which system do you think results in more convictions, or guilty verdicts, and why: civil law as practiced in Europe or common law as practiced in Great Britain and the United States?

2. Compare the advantages of having a judge decide a case without a jury to the advantages of having a jury decide a case.

3. Which principle of law do you think is fairer, "innocent until proven guilty" or "guilty until proven innocent"? Why?

D. Pursuing the Topic

The following are recommended for a closer look at the justice system in the United States:

Books/Periodicals

Posner, Richard A. "Juries on Trial." *Commentary*, March 1995, pp. 49-53.

> *Posner discusses criticism of the American jury system by experts who claim that the sustem is too easy on the defendants in criminal cases and too sympathetic to plaintiffs in civil cases. Recent books suggest that the jury system is likely to end in civil cases.*

Films/Videos

The Verdict, Sidney Lumet, director; 129 minutes, R.

> *This film depicts courtroom drama as a down-and-out Boston lawyer takes on a medical malpractice suit.*

Reversal of Fortune, Barbet Schroeder, director; 120 minutes, R.

> *A Harvard law professor and lawyer attempts to reverse the conviction of a man found guilty of the attempted murder of his wife in this film, which is based on a true story.*

Field Trip

If you are studying in the States, it may be possible for your instructor to make arrangements for your class to visit a local courthouse, where you can watch the proceedings. Virtually all courtroom proceedings are open to the public.

UNIT QUIZ DIRECTIONS

Now that you have completed from one to three chapters in this unit, your teacher may want you to take a quiz on the chapter(s). Your teacher will tell you whether or not you can use your notes to answer the questions on the quiz. If you can use your notes, review them before taking the quiz so that you can anticipate the questions and know where to find the answers. If you cannot use your notes on the quiz, *study them carefully before you take the quiz*, concentrating on organizing the information into main ideas and details that support these main ideas.

Work in small groups to help each other anticipate the questions your teacher will ask. Before breaking up into groups, review your notes and highlight important, noteworthy points. After reviewing your notes, break up into groups. Discuss and write specific short-answer questions and more general essay questions. (For guidelines in writing questions, see the Unit Quiz Directions at the end of Unit 1.)

Write your group's questions on the following pages.

Unit Quiz Preparation

Assign one group member to write down the questions; all members will help plan and compose the questions. For the lecture on the role of government in the economy, write five short-answer questions that can be answered with a few words or one or two sentences. In addition, write two essay questions; word the questions so that they can easily be turned into topic sentences.

Short-Answer Questions

1. _____

   _____

2. _____

   _____

3. _____

   _____

4. _____

   _____

5. _____

   _____

Essay Questions

1. _____

   _____

2. _____

   _____

Follow-up: Write your questions on the board to discuss as a class.

Written follow-up: Prepare for the quiz by writing answers to the questions your class has proposed. You may have abbreviations in your notes, but do not use abbreviations other than standard ones like *U.S.* in your answers.

Unit Quiz Preparation

Assign one group member to write down the questions; all members will help plan and compose the questions. For the lecture on government by constitution, write five short-answer questions that can be answered with a few words or one or two sentences. In addition, write two essay questions; word the questions so that they can easily be turned into topic sentences.

Short-Answer Questions

1. _____

_____

2. _____

_____

3. _____

_____

4. _____

_____

5. _____

_____

Essay Questions

1. _____

_____

2. _____

_____

Follow-up: Write your questions on the board to discuss as a class.

Written follow-up: Prepare for the quiz by writing answers to the questions your class has proposed. You may have abbreviations in your notes, but do not use abbreviations other than standard ones like *U.S.* in your answers.

Unit Quiz Preparation

Assign one group member to write down the questions; all members will help plan and compose the questions. For the lecture on common law and the jury system, write five short-answer questions that can be answered with a few words or one or two sentences. In addition, write two essay questions; word the questions so that they can easily be turned into topic sentences.

Short-Answer Questions

1. _____

   _____

2. _____

   _____

3. _____

   _____

4. _____

   _____

5. _____

   _____

Essay Questions

1. _____

   _____

2. _____

   _____

Follow-up: Write your questions on the board to discuss as a class.

Written follow-up: Prepare for the quiz by writing answers to the questions your class has proposed. You may have abbreviations in your notes, but do not use abbreviations other than standard ones like *U.S.* in your answers.

CREDITS

Photography/Illustration